No Grain
Healthy Brain Cookbook

101 Delicious Low Carb and Gluten-Free Brain Healthy Recipes

TABLE OF CONTENTS

BREAKFASTS

LUNCH

SOUP

APPETIZERS

DINNER

DESSERTS

FOREWORD

Hi, I'm Piper,

I'm a self-confessed foodie; I love cooking and entertaining my family and friends with delicious meals. The kitchen is my favorite place and I'm at my happiest constructing recipes and dishes packed with flavor and fresh ingredients.

Having teenage children and approaching middle age, I recently started assessing my lifestyle and overall health – I wanted to do everything in my power to stay fit and strong in to my late 40s and 50s and through my elderly years, to enjoy a long and happy retirement.

I pored over health and wellness blogs, buried myself in self-help books and consulted nutritionists, life coaches and doctors to get as much guidance on running my body like a well-maintained machine!

After months of research, I came to a realization. There was so much I could do to look after my heart, cleanse my liver, boost my immune system, lose weight and fight disease. But although these things were clearly very important, the picture appeared to be incomplete without a crucial piece of the puzzle, one often overlooked. Brain health.

A healthy brain is the foundation for a healthy body. We spend so much time thinking about the state of our heart, skin, bones, and digestive system – but without a functioning brain, even the fittest person will suffer.

To imagine not achieving the dream of seeing my kids grow older, meeting my grandchildren, or enjoying my husband's company well in to old age if my brain was struck by some debilitating condition such as Alzheimer's disease – that was a devastating thought.

So, came my lightbulb moment to focus on how to best cook for brain health.

You've heard of the phrase 'brain food', right? Well that phrase applies *every* time we eat a meal or a snack; just like the other organs in our body, we are feeding our brain with nutrients and energy to keep it running.

Now, what if we've been unintentionally feeding our brains the wrong food?

I was determined to get to the bottom of this exploration and apply my findings with a deft hand in the kitchen.

Research quickly led me to find out that most brain disorders are caused by inflammation – when the body suffers an inflammatory response, it triggers the same in the brain, and over time this can lead to devastating cognitive disorders. And here's where I had my second 'lightbulb' moment – can you guess which two food groups are most responsible for the highest rate of inflammation in the body?

The first? Glutens. And the second? Carbohydrates; specifically of the high GI kind.

As I'm sure you are aware, glutens are found in foods containing wheat, barley and rye, which usually includes breads and pastas, cakes and even beer to name a few. Glutens stimulate inflammation, and the scary thing is, while usually this inflammation can be diagnosed in most parts of the body (such as through irritable bowel syndrome, bloating, and gut issues), its effects on the brain can go largely unnoticed.

So the grains had to go. And while I was getting tough on food elimination, I found that to complete the picture, I needed to team the no gluten ethos with a low carb diet.

Carbohydrates are found in many grain foods anyway, but they're also lurking in sugary desserts, starchy vegetables, and high GI fruits.

Carbs are famous for raising blood sugar levels and stimulating insulin, which affects the body's ability to burn fat.

So my mission had begun; to put my family and I on a gluten-free, low-carb diet and start consciously maintaining our bodies for life. Everyone complained at first, thinking they would have to eat boring and tasteless

meals – but I promised to find a way to make food that was not only good for us, but that also tasted amazing!

My research and experimentation began and I soon discovered there was plenty of information out there – we were far from alone in our specific dietary requirements. I started putting together recipes. It was exciting to go to the grocery store with new eyes, and easier than I expected to find everything we needed.

I almost didn't recognize my pantry as it was stocked full of new and intriguing ingredients. The experimenting was well underway. I discovered a great selection of gluten-free alternative flours to whip up breads and cakes, pancakes and pizza crusts.

And sugar was easily replaced with stevia and erythritol options that were negligible in carbohydrates and barely registered on the glycemic index.

It seemed that almost every recipe could be substituted and flavor wasn't suffering at all!

First I baked a loaf of gluten-free bread, and I was pleasantly surprised at how delicious it tasted – this was only the beginning. Through research, trial and error I built a recipe portfolio of our family favorites, all completely gluten-free and light on carbs. I created soups, tikka masala, pot roasts, fish, and chicken dishes.

And let's not forget the sweet stuff! Brownies, muffins, cookies and cakes all came out of my kitchen, wheat, gluten and sugar free yet easily satisfying our love for desserts.

I discovered that as well as cutting gluten and carbs, another treat for the brain and body is to increase our fat intake. With the carbohydrates low, the fats weren't adding to weight gain, and 'good fats' like avocado, olive oil, nuts and seeds proved to be excellent lubricators for brain function.

You'll find these ingredients and more in many of my recipes.

101 Delicious Low Carb, Gluten-Free Brain Healthy Recipes

The transformation in my family and I after a few weeks was like day and night. We lost pounds in weight. Our energy levels soared, despite all being busy people. I slept like a baby for the first time in years. Everyone reported to feeling clearer and brighter. And that was just on the outside – imagine the changes going on in our bodies and brains!

Now when I cook for the family or invite guests over, I continue to make gluten-free low-carb dishes for every course. Not a hint of wheat, barley, rye or high GI carbs to be found in any meal. The best part is, everyone loves it and nobody knows the difference, because the food tastes fantastic and leaves you feeling good.

What they don't know… is recipes like these may in fact help them live a longer life and feel better.

I started out on this journey wanting to safeguard my future health, and I've ended up creating a whole book of tasty gluten-free, low-carb recipes that allow us to enjoy our favorite foods and still feel good.

So, whether you've had the same fears as me and want to make a change or you're just looking for some tasty new recipes, come and enjoy the pleasure of gluten-free low-carb cooking on a journey through 101 breakfast, lunch, dinner and dessert recipes that have transformed my family and friend's lives into healthier and happier people.

I know you're going to love what comes out of your kitchen, and your health will thank you for it!

Piper

IMPORTANT FOR CELIACS

Although we are trying to decrease inflammation with a reduction in carbs, we are also looking at staying gluten-free.

For some of us, a gluten-free lifestyle is not only a healthy lifestyle choice, but also an absolute necessity.

Staying strict on gluten is great, anyway, however for any celiacs reading this, before we begin, over the next few pages, I want to give you a list of considerations on some ingredients you may come across in the recipes ahead.

Most seasoned wheat and gluten 'avoidees' wouldn't normally need to have all of this information spelled out, nevertheless it's worthwhile repeating here.

You'll notice that a recurring theme in the below list to follow is when purchasing ingredients for any recipe always read ingredient labels of anything ambiguous or that you are unsure of, for peace of mind that you are in fact buying a wheat/gluten free product.

As you may well be aware, there are sometimes cross-contamination issues with many products, and often hidden additives that contain gluten and wheat. A prime example would be soy sauce, which can contain wheat to thicken it.

Following is a list of notable ingredients included in some recipes in this book, with notes and suggestions on how you should approach the selection process when stocking your shelves with these products.

Ultimately, the onus is on you to do your due diligence, so in addition to these suggestions, please do double check any ingredients in a recipe you are preparing to ensure you are eating gluten-free!

Happy eating!

GLUTEN-FREE INGREDIENT CONSIDERATIONS

BEVERAGES

Coffee

Stick to plain and unflavored coffee and you should be fine - some brands can risk cross contamination, and can cause some digestive issues with some celiacs, so label checking is always a good idea.

Spirits

A source of debate, some celiac sufferers can handle drinking scotch or whiskey or vodka or other spirits without any issues despite their gluten sensitivity.

Others are sensitive and have reported gluten reactions if the spirit is distilled from gluten-based grains. Look for alternatives if this is the case, such as potato distilled vodka.

Whey Protein Powder

Not all of these specialist powdered drinks can be assumed to be gluten free or low carb so labels need to be checked accordingly if included in a recipe.

Wine

Wine is another contentious ingredient – it may contain a marginal amount of gluten from the brewers yeast, or if wheat gluten has been used for finning or clarifying agents, or from the paste used in sealing the wooden casks. Also colorings and flavorings may contain wheat.

Many people never report any sensitivity. Thankfully some wineries are advertising their wines as gluten free so if you have any concerns, look for these before enjoying a drop.

BISCUITS & CHIPS

Shortbread Biscuits / Tortilla, Natural or Original Potato Chips

You must always check the label of these to ensure that these are gluten free – even if it the item makes claims of 'healthy' or 'heart smart' or 'yeast free'.

Of course, these are not considered low carb so should have little place on your shelf anyway!

CONDIMENTS

Horseradish

Horseradish is the root of a plant, so our main concerns are cross-contamination during manufacture or any other ingredients added such as vinegar. However, very few commercially prepared horseradish sauces are labeled 'gluten free', so stay diligent and do a label check.

Ketchup / Tomato Paste

Ketchup is often gluten-free but this is not always the case, due to the addition of vinegar. Heinz is often reported as being a safe bet. Do your own due diligence as per usual, and watch out you don't cross contaminate the ketchup with a bready knife.

Mayonnaise

Most mayonnaise contains soy, which can be cross contaminated with gluten, so again, you should look for gluten free labels to be safe. Or why not make your own?

Mustard

Most mustards, Dijon and French mustard are generally ok – as long as distilled grain or malt vinegar or wheat flour have not been added to it which happens sometimes to keep costs down – as always check the label.

Soy Sauce

Many brands contain wheat-based gluten as a thickener and this is something you should check for. I always recommend you look for the gluten free info on the label before purchasing.

Worcestershire Sauce

Many are not gluten-free so you'll need to look for a certified gluten-free option here.

DAIRY / SOY / TOFU

Butter

Plain and unsalted are usually gluten free. Check the label to avoid pesky gluten bearing additives.

Cheese

Our friends are the aged hard cheeses and are usually gluten free and good to go – (think Cheddar, Swiss, Parmesan).

We need to check the ingredients list on the soft cheeses (Cottage, Cream and all pasteurized, and processed). Avoid those with vegetable gums, food starches and preservatives not defined by a gluten-free source.

Oh, and it's worth a mention that Ricotta and Mozzarella contain vinegar, which isn't always gluten free. (see vinegar in this list).

Eggs

When a chicken has been fed a heavy diet of gluten grains, the eggs produced can affect a very sensitive individual. As a rule eggs are ok, but be aware eggs may contain the tiniest traces of gluten.

Margarine

Most margarine is ok and gluten free, but when in doubt, check the label as always. At any rate, butter is better.

Milk

The good news is that cows milk doesn't contain gluten, but you should know that if you are on a gluten free diet because of Celiac Disease, you might have trouble with digesting the milk at first until the small intestine takes some time out to repair itself. If this is the case, either keep it at bay for a while, or try some Lactase before you drink the milk to see if that helps.

Regarding soy milks, almond milks and dry milk/buttermilk powders some of these may have had gluten or modified food starches added to them, so as always, double check all labels.

Sour cream

Sour cream is generally gluten free unless it has had additives included.

Yogurt

All natural, soy and plain (unflavored/unsweetened) yogurts should be gluten free. Check the label to be sure, some brands have flavored options as gluten free too if you can find them.

Tofu

You will almost always be ok with plain tofu. Keep in mind that some tofu is flavored and may not be gluten-free depending on the compounds used, such as soy sauce made with wheat. Reading the label is always a good habit!

EXTRACTS & BASICS

Caramel

True caramel should be gluten free, but be careful and check labels, as artificial caramel can sometimes be colored from a variety of products that are common allergens such as glucose (wheat base), malt (barley base) and lactose (dairy based). Most US companies use corn though.

Cocoa & Cocoa Extract

All pure, dark cocoa and cocoa extract should be gluten-free. Hot cocoa mix needs to be checked to make sure nothing like malt has been added.

Curry Paste

Curry paste may have non gluten-free thickeners added – check the ingredients before purchasing.

Dark Chocolate

Again, you'll need to check to make sure is this is specifically marked gluten free. And then once you discover one that is, you may need to do some chocolate tasting tests! Purely for science of course!

Herbs & Spices

There are many mixed herbs and spices included in the recipes in this book, such as nutmeg and cayenne pepper, paprika, cinnamon, ginger, cumin, turmeric, coriander, garam masala, oregano etc.

Please be aware that some brands may contain flour to prevent clumping and labels should be checked. You can usually find what you need in markets or organic stores.

Oils

Pure olive oils, canola, corn, sesame and safflower oils are generally gluten free.

In some rare cases of extreme sensitivity, sunflower oil that has been harvested by the same equipment as wheat can cause issues for a severe celiac or gluten intolerant person.

Also, check the label to ensure no additional additives will trip you up.

In this book, I have recommended olive and coconut oils, suited for a healthy brain!

Stock

Chicken, lamb, fish and vegetable broths and stocks, must be clearly labelled gluten free before you buy. Check the ingredients for wheat, rye, or barley.

Vanilla / Alcohol-Based Extracts

There should be no reason to avoid flavoring extracts, such as vanilla extract, because they contain distilled alcohol, Pure distilled alcohol is gluten free regardless of the starting material.

However, I'd refer you to the above note on 'Spirits' if you have any problems here. Some brands are marked gluten-free for peace of mind.

Vinegar

Vinegar derived from gluten grains, such as distilled white vinegar, can definitely be a problem for a substantial minority of celiacs regardless of the distillation process, (my husband Evan is among these).

Malt vinegar is not distilled so avoid this completely.

Most should be ok with apple cider vinegar, wine vinegar, cane vinegar, and rice vinegar that contains no other grains. Most balsamic vinegar is ok but keep in mind that the paste that seals the casks is often wheat based, but it's a very trace amount that would ever find its way to the product. Just so you are aware.

Yeast

Yeast is naturally gluten free but some brands do have added wheat so again, check the labels. As a rule avoid brewers yeast.

FLOURS & STARCH

In the recipes ahead, we have not only prioritized gluten-free but also, low-carb, so this section is barely relevant! However, here is the skinny on staying gluten-free with flours and starches.

Baking Powder

Baking powder could have gluten in it. It's a mixture of baking soda, cream of tartar, and usually, but not always, cornstarch.

It's possible that the starch used could be something else containing gluten, although normally in the U.S. it isn't. Read the labels and investigate accordingly.

Baking Soda

Should be naturally gluten free, unless it has some fillers in it, which would be unusual!

Corn Starch

While pure corn starch by itself is gluten free, wheat flour is sometimes added in order to enhance the binding power for baking purposes. You should check the label to see if it specifically says "gluten free", especially since some brands are made in facilities that share equipment with wheat products, causing cross contamination issues.

Be doubly aware if in Australia, that "cornflour" was once made of wheat, as wheat was the dominantly available grain. It's a confusing one, but nothing a moment reading the label can't clear up.

Cornmeal

Again, you should be ok but cross contamination can be an issue. You may want to check labels for statements like "processed on equipment or a facility that also processes wheat".

Specialised Flours

As a rule, many specialized flours are all gluten free:

Rice flour, Potato flour, Buckwheat flour, Chickpea flour, Sorghum flour, Quinoa flour, Bean flour, Fava flour, Potato starch, and Tapioca flour to name a few that are included in the recipes to follow.

There are some caveats. Wheat flour is sometimes added to some flour mixes. There can be issues of cross contamination.

These flours are great to have in the kitchen, just check carefully for any type of wheat product in the ingredients list and check if the label specifically says "gluten free".

FRUIT & NUTS

Most fruits are bursting with high GI carbs (a few berries are ok though), so will be omitted from this book. In general though, when eating fruit gluten won't be a huge consideration, but let me say something about bananas...

Bananas

Bananas in and of themselves, are gluten free. This is a tricky one. It has been hypothesized that the protein lectin which is found in bananas can in some individuals be confused by the body for gluten, and could cause a reaction, as could the fructose. There has been reports that the riper the banana the less chance of tummy trouble.

Because of this issue, if you already know or find that eating bananas causes you issues such as problems with your digestion, you may want to avoid these recipes, or substitute the fruit

Nuts, Seeds and By-Products (including Coconut)

Pure unflavored nuts, and many seeds such as flax, pumpkin, poppy, and sunflower are gluten free. Watch for cross-contamination in packaging, or shelf displays.

Take care with any unusual ingredients in nut flours, and butters and look for statements on the packaging such as "may contain wheat".

MEAT

Bacon

Read the label. Not all bacon products will be gluten free as it depends on any marination or spices that have been used to season and flavor the product.

PULSES, BEANS AND LENTILS

Dry Beans and Lentils

These may contain gluten from cross contamination and will usually be marked on the packaging. Canned is usually a safer source in this respect. As always check the label.

RICE & GRAINS

If you ever choose to included these in a recipe, however uncommon these choices may be on a low-carb, gluten free diet, remember this.

Oats

When you are choosing oats, ensure you are buying the gluten free version as they can often be cross contaminated by wheat crops.

Even this may not be enough with oats however. The other main issue is that oats contain a protein that is very similar to the gluten protein called avenin. Around 10% of celiac sufferers still get a reaction from the avenin and should avoid eating oats if this occurs. You may well already know the answer to this!

Polenta

Polenta is a gluten free food, again be aware of potential for cross-contaminated products, check labels, and if possible buy gluten-free.

Rice

Rice flour, rice syrup, and puffed rice cereal are all considered gluten free however they are all subject to cross contamination and labels need to be checked accordingly.

BREAKFASTS

BREAKY BUN

A handy recipe for a breakfast bun which you could top with any low carb gluten-free treat such as melted cheese, a slice of bacon or some chopped green onion. They are also good just as they are, spread with some butter.

Makes 6

INGREDIENTS:

1½ ounces coconut flour

3½ ounces flaxseed meal

½ tsp. salt

3 tsp. baking powder

2 tbsp. butter, melted

6 large fresh eggs, beaten

DIRECTIONS:

1. Pre-heat the oven to 350°F.

2. Grease a large cookie sheet or cover it with non-stick parchment paper.

3. In a large bowl mix together the coconut flour, ground flaxseed, salt and baking powder.

4. Pour in the melted butter and rub the ingredients together with your hands to form breadcrumbs.

5. Add the eggs to the mixture and mix well together.

6. Place spoonfuls onto the baking sheet, well apart.

7. The mixture will be quite loose.

8. Place in the oven and bake for 15 – 20 minutes until brown.

9. Leave to cool on the cookie sheet for about 5 minutes before transferring to a wire rack to cool completely.

CHEESE AND MUSHROOM SOUFFLE OMELET

This omelet has a creamy mushroom center and is easily tweaked with different fillings.

Serves 2

INGREDIENTS:

2 medium fresh eggs

1 tbsp. cold water

¼ cup full fat cream cheese

2 ounces mushrooms, chopped

1 tbsp. butter

1 tsp. fresh parsley, chopped finely

Salt and pepper (to taste)

Paprika or cayenne pepper (to garnish)

DIRECTIONS:

1. Heat half of the butter in a small skillet and sauté the mushrooms until tender.

2. Set aside to cool.

3. Beat the cream cheese adding the chopped parsley along with the cooled mushrooms. Season to taste.

4. Preheat a broiler to high.

5. Heat the rest of the butter in a small clean skillet

6. Break the eggs into as small bowl and whisk together with the water and some seasoning until fluffy.

7. Pour the egg mixture into the skillet and cook the omelet gently by lifting the sides and allowing the uncooked egg to go underneath.

8. When nearly set, place the omelet under the hot broiler where it will puff up and cook in the centre.

9. Remove from the broiler, slide out of the skillet onto a plate.

10. Spoon over the cream cheese mixture and garnish with paprika or cayenne.

11. Fold over if desired. Cut in half and serve.

12. Eat while still hot.

CINNAMON FLAPJACKS

Sunday morning Brunch! Serve with sugar free maple syrup!

Makes 18

INGREDIENTS:

3 large fresh eggs

4½ tablespoons full fat coconut cream.

1 small ripe banana

1 teaspoon lemon juice

1 teaspoon vanilla extract

3 tablespoons coconut flour

1 teaspoon cinnamon

½ teaspoon baking soda

Pinch sea salt.

Coconut oil for cooking

DIRECTIONS:

1. Peel and mash the banana.

2. In a large jug thoroughly beat together the eggs, coconut cream, mashed banana, lemon juice and vanilla extract.

3. Combine the dry ingredients in a separate bowl.

4. Heat the coconut oil in a non stick pan over a medium heat.

5. Beat the dry ingredients into the egg mixture.

6. Pour about a tablespoon of batter onto the heated pan. Put several side by side leaving a space to spread.

7. Cook on the underneath and when bubbles begin to form and rise to the surface of the flapjack.

8. Turn over carefully with a spatula to cook on the other side.

9. Remove to a dry clean kitchen towel to cool while you are cooking the rest of the mixture.

Indeed a delicious and versatile addition to your healthy brain recipe repertoire!

FRESH BLUEBERRY MUFFINS

You can make these with blueberries or strawberries too, whatever takes your fancy!

Makes 20

INGREDIENTS:

2 cups almond flour

1 teaspoon baking soda

1 teaspoon baking powder

½ teaspoon sea salt

1 teaspoon pure almond extract

6 fresh farm eggs

2 cups almond butter

½ cup erythritol

½ cup slivered almonds

¾ cup coconut oil, melted

2 cups fresh blueberries

DIRECTIONS:

1. Preheat your oven to 350°F.

2. Prepare 20 muffin cups by lining with paper cases.

3. Mix all dry ingredients together in a large bowl.

4. Whisk the eggs, almond butter, erythritol, almonds, almond extract and coconut oil together in another bowl

5. Add the dry ingredients to the wet ingredients and mix lightly until just combined

6. Gently fold through the fresh blueberries.

7. Divide the muffin mixture equally among the prepared muffin

cups.

8. Bake for 18 - 22 minutes.

9. Turn the muffins after baking for 15 minutes and check that they do not overcook.

10. Leave to cool for a while after removing from the oven.

Eat these warm while fresh from the oven – so good for any time of the day when those hunger pangs get the better of you!

NUTTY BREAKFAST MUFFINS

Muffins for breakfast – yum! These muffins may be frozen and reheated in the microwave for an easy breakfast option. Top with some chopped macadamias if you like.

Makes 8

INGREDIENTS:

1⅓ cups fine almond flour

⅔ cup fine flaxseed meal

¾ tsp. baking powder

1 tsp. powdered cinnamon

½ tsp. baking soda

¼ tsp. salt

¾ cup unsweetened coconut, shredded

1¼ cups erythritol

2½ ounces butter, melted

1½ tsp vanilla extract

3 tbsp. heavy cream

2½ tbsp. water

2 large fresh farm eggs, beaten

DIRECTIONS:

1. Preheat the oven to 350°F.
2. Line 8 muffin cups with paper muffin cases.
3. In a medium sized bowl, thoroughly mix together the almond flour, flaxseed meal, baking powder, baking soda, cinnamon and salt.
4. Add the coconut and sugar substitute.

5. In a separate bowl, mix together the melted butter, vanilla, cream and water.

6. Beat into the eggs.

7. Add this liquid mixture to the dry ingredients and mix well together.

8. Spoon this mixture evenly among the muffin cups.

9. Bake for 18 – 20 minutes until brown and the mixture is cooked. Test with a toothpick if necessary.

10. Cook for a few minutes longer if needed.

11. Remove from the oven and cook on a cake rack for a few minutes before removing the muffins from the cups.

RASPBERRY SWIRL PANCAKES

Different, delicious and sure to leave you craving more!

Makes 12 pancakes

INGREDIENTS:

2 cups fresh raspberries – pick your own if you can

4 tablespoons freshly squeezed lemon juice

4 tablespoons erythritol

1 tablespoon sugar free syrup

6 large fresh farm eggs

1¼ cups unsweetened almond milk

1 tablespoon sugar free maple syrup

2 teaspoons vanilla extract

1½ cup coconut flour

½ cup tapioca flour

2 teaspoons baking powder

Pinch sea salt

DIRECTIONS:

1. In a saucepan set on a medium heat, make a thick puree with the raspberries, lemon juice, syrup and erythritol. Be careful it does not burn by stirring regularly and turning the heat down to low.

2. Whisk together the eggs, almond milk, syrup and vanilla in a large bowl.

3. Add the flours, baking powder and salt a little at a time, whisking well between additions.

4. Whisk to a smooth thick cream consistency.

5. Set a large skillet over a medium heat and grease with a little

coconut oil to get hot.

6. Using a ladle pour flapjack sized pancakes into the pan. Place a small spoon full of the raspberry mixture on the top of each and gentle swirl.

7. Leave until bubbles form on the top. Flip and cook on the other side.

8. Repeat with the rest of the mixture.

9. Cool on a kitchen towel and eat while fresh.

SMOKED SALMON SCRAMBLE

This breakfast dish is packed with protein from the egg scramble to irresistible salmon strips. If you love salmon, you will enjoy this!

Serves 2

INGREDIENTS:

4 medium eggs, beaten

1/2 tsp. dried mixed herbs

1 tbsp. butter

2 tbsp. cream

Ground black pepper

DIRECTIONS:

1. In a bowl, mix the cream, eggs, herbs and butter. Season to taste.

2. Add to a medium saucepan heated over medium heat and scramble the eggs.

3. Arrange the strips of the smoked salmon on a plate on top of the scrambled eggs. Add a dash of freshly ground pepper.

4. Serve warm and enjoy!

SPANISH OMELETTE

Hola huevos! Usted es muy delicioso con carne! (It's true, these taste great).

Serves 4

INGREDIENTS:

8 eggs

4 ounces spicy ground beef

4 ounces cheddar cheese, shredded

4 tbsp. salsa

½ avocado, sliced

4 tbsp. sour cream

2 tbsp. black olives, sliced

1 jalapeno pickled pepper, sliced

¼ cup chopped cilantro

DIRECTIONS:

1. In a bowl, beat the eggs and pour them into a large pre-heated non-stick skillet.

2. Leave the egg to set and form an omelette.

3. Sprinkle over the beef, cheese and salsa.

4. Fold the omelette over and cut into 4 large pieces.

5. Place each piece on a serving plate and top each with a quarter of the avocado, 1 tbsp. sour cream.

6. Sprinkle each serving with olives, pepper and cilantro.

STRAWBERRY PANCAKES

This sweet pancake recipe will quickly become one of your favorites. Feel free to change the berries if you want to get creative, or halve the berries to go a little stricter on the carb intake.

Makes 8

INGREDIENTS:

¾ cup coconut milk

½ cup water

¼ cup unsweetened almond milk

1½ tsp. baking powder

½ cup coconut flour

¼ cup almond flour

1 tsp. cinnamon

3 drops liquid stevia extract (adjust to taste)

6 eggs

½ cup fresh strawberries

Butter for cooking

Sugar free syrup to serve

DIRECTIONS:

1. Sieve the flours, baking powder and cinnamon together in a large bowl.

2. Beat together the eggs, coconut milk, water, stevia drops and almond milk.

3. Add the egg mixture slowly to the flour, beating well so that no lumps are formed.

4. Heat a little butter in a large skillet and drop tablespoons of batter onto it when hot.

5.   Put a few strawberries into the batter before it sets.

6.   Allow to set on the base before flipping over and cooking the top for a few moments.

7.   Remove from the skillet and keep warm in a clean tea towel while cooking the rest.

8.   Serve with sugar free syrup and enjoy.

ZESTY CRAB CAKES

Enjoy these on a sunny summer's day! They are served with a tangy mayo dressing too.

Serves 6

INGREDIENTS:

1 pound crab meat, shredded

¼ cup olive oil

¼ cup flax seed flour

3 tbsp. coconut flour

1 tsp. salt

1 tsp. mustard powder

1 tsp. garlic powder

Pinch freshly ground black pepper

2 small celery stalks, finely chopped

½ red bell pepper, finely chopped

4 small green onion, minced

2 large fresh eggs

1½ tbsp. Worcestershire sauce

Butter for frying

Chili sauce to taste

DIRECTIONS:

1. In a large bowl mix together all of the ingredients (except for the chili sauce and butter), to make a firm dough.

2. With damp hands form the mixture into 12 small patties and flatten to about ½ inch (1.25cm) thick.

3. Heat some butter in skillet and fry the crab cakes in batches until brown and cooked through. About 5 minutes each side.

4. Serve hot with chili sauce to your taste.

LUNCH

ADUKI BEAN STIR FRY

A sure-fire hit featuring combined fresh vegetables. Nothing beats a quick meal packed with a generous serving of nutrition.

Serves 8 generously

INGREDIENTS:

18 ounces winter cabbage, cored and shredded

8 ounces Aduki beans, cooked

1 inch piece fresh ginger, peeled and finely chopped

2 cloves garlic, diced

1 tbsp. gluten-free soy sauce

1 tbsp. extra virgin olive oil

1 tbsp. sesame oil

DIRECTIONS:

1. Rinse the cabbage and drain well.

2. Heat a large frying pan. Pour in the olive oil and lightly fry the ginger and garlic.

3. Add the cabbage to the frying pan and stir fry for about 4-5 minutes. Avoid burning the cabbage.

4. Mix in the Aduki beans and stir fry until well heated.

5. Drizzle with sesame oil and soy sauce and mix and toss well, blending and distributing the flavors equally.

6. Serve hot.

AVOCADO, TOMATO & 2 CHEESE SALAD

A deliciously easy salad to add a sparkle to your day. So quick to prepare.

Serves 4

INGREDIENTS:

4 medium avocados, peeled and sliced

6 small ripe tomatoes, skinned and chopped

1 small red onion, finely chopped

1 cup fresh basil leaves, torn

3 ounces mozzarella cheese, broken into bite sized pieces

3 ounces Cheddar cheese, shaved

¼ cup extra virgin olive oil

2 tsp. white wine vinegar

Salt and pepper to taste

DIRECTIONS:

1. Toss the avocado, tomatoes and onion together lightly.

2. Sprinkle with the oil and vinegar and lightly toss again.

3. Cover and refrigerate for 30 minutes for the flavors to mingle.

4. Remove from the refrigerator and add the cheeses.

5. Spoon carefully into serve bowls.

6. Top with the torn basil leaves.

BEEF AND MUSHROOM STIR-FRY

A quick and easy dish to prepare for lunch.

Serves 6

INGREDIENTS:

2 tbsp. olive oil

1 large onion, finely sliced

1 large bell pepper, seeded and sliced

10 ounces portobello mushrooms, sliced

1 small green cabbage, coarsely shredded

8 ounces small broccoli florets

1 pound rump or fillet steak, sliced into thin strips

2 tbsp. light soy sauce

2 tsp. powdered Chinese five spice

Salt and pepper to season

DIRECTIONS:

1. Heat the oil in a large skillet or wok over a high heat.

2. Add the onions and stir fry for a few minutes until translucent.

3. Add the bell pepper, broccoli and the mushrooms and fry for a minute or so.

4. Add the beef steak and fry until it is brown.

5. Stir in the cabbage and toss everything together.

6. Pour over the soy sauce, sprinkle the spice over the dish and mix everything together well.

7. Season with salt and pepper.

8. Serve whilst still hot and the vegetables remain crispy.

CAULIFLOWER SALAD

A tender cauliflower salad with a healthy twist! Add chopped red bell pepper and chili for extra color and a zing.

Serves 4

INGREDIENTS:

1 head cauliflower, broken into florets

2 stalks celery, diced

4 tablespoons finely chopped red onion

1 tablespoon finely chopped parsley

2 tablespoons olive oil

1 tablespoon Dijon mustard

½ teaspoon sea salt

DIRECTIONS:

1. Steam the cauliflower until just tender. Allow to cool and then place in a large bowl.

2. Add the celery, onion and parsley.

3. Whisk together the olive oil, mustard and salt.

4. Pour over the cauliflower.

5. Leave in the fridge for an hour or so for the flavors to develop.

6. Serve.

CELERY AND BEETROOT SALAD

A delicious salad with a tangy lemon dressing! This salad does not keep and it needs to be eaten as soon as it is made however with a flavor combo like this, that shouldn't be a problem.

Serves 6

INGREDIENTS:

1 bunch arugula (salad rocket)

1 bunch watercress

1 large cooked beetroot

1 small celery root

1 green apple

1 small red onion

⅓ cup freshly squeezed lemon juice

2 tablespoons roasted garlic purée

1 tablespoon Dijon mustard

1 tablespoon sugar free maple syrup

¼ cup extra virgin olive oil

¼ cup flax oil

½ cup coarsely chopped pecans

Salt and pepper to taste

DIRECTIONS:

1. Wash the arugula and watercress and remove any coarse stems. Allow to soak in cold water while preparing the rest of the salad.

2. Peel the beetroot, celery and apple and cut each one into this julienne strips or grate them coarsely on a grater.

3. Cut the onion into this slices

4. Combine all of the remaining ingredients, except for the pecans, and whisk together in a large bowl until emulsified.

5. Add the vegetable strips and toss until well coated. Leave for a few minutes for the flavors to combine.

6. Drain the greens and pat gently to dry or use a salad spinner.

7. Add the vegetables and toss everything well together.

8. Sprinkle walnuts on top and serve.

GRILLED AVOCADOS STUFFED WITH CHICKEN

A taste sensation!

Serves 1 for each avocado

INGREDIENTS:

1 ripe avocado per person

Chopped cooked chicken, fish or meat of your choice

Chopped tomatoes

Roasted chopped red or yellow bell peppers (save the juice formed when they are roasting!)

Cumin powder

Freshly squeezed lime or lemon juice

Salt and pepper

Cilantro lime ranch dressing and chopped fresh cilantro to serve

DIRECTIONS:

1. Cut the avocado in half lengthways and remove the seed.

2. Hollow out the fruit a little with a spoon to make a slightly larger cavity (Use the excess flesh in a salad or as guacamole).

3. Mix together the chopped ingredients and mix with some freshly squeezed citrus juice, bell pepper juice and cumin in a bowl.

4. Add salt and pepper to taste.

5. Stuff the hollowed out avocado with this mixture

6. Place over a medium barbeque for about 5 minutes (Do not flip over as they will lose their contents!) after which place under a broiler for another 4 minutes. Make sure that you cook both sides.

7. Top with cilantro lime dressing and chopped cilantro.

SEAFOOD SALAD WITH A DASH OF LIME

A combination of haddock, prawns, chili, red onion, and seasonings! A creative and tasty combination!

Serves 4

INGREDIENTS:

22 ounces fresh, or frozen haddock fillets, skinned and boned

1 large mild red chili, halved and seeded

½ a small red onion, peeled and minced

1½ cups of fresh shrimp, shells removed

Salt and freshly ground black pepper

1 large lemon, juiced

3 limes, juiced and zested

4 tbsp. vodka

2 tbsp. olive oil

3 ounces prepared lambs lettuce

Cilantro leaves to garnish

DIRECTIONS:

1. Cut the fish into strips and chop the chili.

2. Place the fish, chili, onion, salt, prawns, pepper, lemon juice, lime juice, vodka and oil in a large dish and mix thoroughly.

3. Leave overnight to marinate covered with plastic wrap.

4. Put the fish and its juices on a serving plate along with the lambs lettuce. Sprinkle with cilantro.

5. Serve the salad on individual plates.

THAI GREEN CURRY

Eastern flavors abound with pork, coconut and lime. A lunch tasty enough to serve to transport your tastebuds to Thailand!

Serves 4

INGREDIENTS:

1½ ounces shallot, finely chopped

¼ cup olive oil

16 ounces fresh pork, diced

1 tsp. fresh ginger, grated

2 tsp. Thai green curry paste

14½ ounces chicken broth

13½ ounces full cream coconut milk

Salt to taste

2 green onions, sliced diagonally

½ cup fresh basil, shredded

1 tbsp. freshly squeezed lime juice

DIRECTIONS:

1. Heat the oil in a large skillet or wok over a high heat.

2. Add the shallots and pork and stir fry until brown and nearly cooked.

3. Turn down the heat and add the ginger and curry paste. Stir to make sure the meat is evenly coated.

4. Add the broth, coconut milk and salt to taste.

5. Bring to the boil and reduce by a half, about 15 minutes.

6. Stir in the green onions, basil and lime juice.

7. Serve in individual bowls.

THREE CHEESE STUFFED CHICKEN BREASTS

A perfect treat for the whole family! Chicken breasts just oozing rich, lush cheese and filling your home with a fantastic smell.

Serves 6

INGREDIENTS:

6 chicken breasts, skinned and boned

½ cup ricotta cheese

½ cup Gruyere cheese, finely shredded

1 tsp. fresh thyme, finely chopped

1 tsp. fresh parsley, finely chopped

½ cup sundried tomatoes in olive oil, diced

12 baby spinach leaves, torn

6 slices mozzarella cheese (optional)

Salt and pepper to season

Powdered paprika to garnish

DIRECTIONS:

1. Pre-heat the oven to 375°F.

2. Carefully slice open each chicken breast, with a sharp knife, to make a pocket in each one.

3. Have ready an ovenproof dish large enough to hold the chicken breasts, side by side.

4. In a medium sized bowl mix together the rest of the ingredients except the mozzarella cheese and the garnish.

5. Divide the cheese mixture into 6 and spoon each serve into the pockets made in the chicken breasts.

6. Secure each opening with one or two toothpicks to hold the filling inside.

44

7. Lay the chicken breasts into the dish and top each one with a slice of mozzarella cheese if using.

8. Place the dish in the hot oven and bake for 35 - 40 minutes uncovered.

9. Check that the chicken is cooked and brown on the top.

10. Serve.

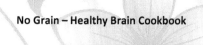

SOUP

BROCCOLI AND GINGER SOUP

A delicious vegetable soup which is best served lukewarm! Flavorful and utterly repeatable!

Serves 4

INGREDIENTS:

½ head of broccoli

2 hearts of celery

4 tomatoes

2 red bell peppers

3 inch piece fresh ginger root

½ small shallot

½ cup coconut water

4 tablespoons fresh lime juice

1 teaspoon cumin

1 teaspoon curry powder

1 teaspoon salt

Pinch cayenne pepper

Extra virgin olive oil to serve

DIRECTIONS:

1. Blend together all of the vegetables.
2. Add the spices to taste.
3. Warm the soup in a saucepan until just warm.
4. Add the coconut water and lime juice.
5. Serve in glasses with a little olive oil drizzled on the top.

BUTTERNUT APPLE SOUP

Another soup to serve lukewarm, with apples and butternut as the core ingredients! This soup has a delicate sweet flavor!

Serves 4

INGREDIENTS:

1 peeled and seeded large butternut squash

2 large green apples, cored

2 medium carrots, grated

½ small red onion

1 cup coconut water

1 teaspoon sea salt

½ teaspoon ground cinnamon

½ teaspoon freshly ground nutmeg

Extra virgin olive oil to serve

DIRECTIONS:

1. Place all of the vegetables and the apple in a blender and blend until smooth.

2. Pour into a saucepan and warm through.

3. Add the flavorings and the coconut water.

4. Taste for seasoning.

5. Serve in glasses with the olive oil drizzled on top.

DELICIOUS AND QUICK BROCCOLI AND CHICKPEA SOUP

Get your spoon ready to dive into this combination of chickpeas and broccoli in a garlic broth.

Serves 5

INGREDIENTS:

1 tsp. olive oil

5 cups gluten-free vegetable broth

¼ cup lemon juice

1½ cup cooked chickpeas

6 cloves of garlic, minced

2 medium broccoli heads, cut in small florets (about 5 cups)

Ground black pepper

DIRECTIONS:

1. Heat the oil in a large pan over a medium-high heat. Sauté the garlic for about 30 seconds. Turn the heat to high and add the broccoli and broth.

2. Cook for 10 minutes and then add the lemon juice and chickpeas.

3. Season with pepper and continue cooking for about 5 – 10 minutes until the broccoli florets are softened and chickpeas are heated through.

4. Serve and enjoy!

PUMPKIN SOUP DELIGHT

Warm yourself from the inside out with this healthy and delicious soup that will surely satisfy your senses! A pumpkin soup that naturally brings out best the sweet sultry taste of fall flavors.

Serves 6

INGREDIENTS:

½ tsp. powdered ginger

2 tbsp. sugar free maple syrup

Ground black pepper and salt

4 cups gluten-free vegetable broth

7½ cups pumpkin puree

6 cups coconut milk (4 tbsp. reserved)

Pumpkin seeds to serve.

DIRECTIONS:

1. In a large pot mix together the pumpkin purée, coconut milk, vegetable broth, syrup and ginger.

2. Bring to the boil over a medium heat, stirring constantly.

3. When the soup starts bubbling, turn the heat down into a simmer. Simmer for about 15 minutes.

4. Add pepper and salt to taste and serve.

5. Garnish each bowl with the reserved coconut milk and sprinkle with pumpkin seeds.

SHRIMP, CHILI AND CUCUMBER SOUP

It's hard to go wrong with a shrimp dish. This recipe combines cucumbers and chilies with shrimp which creates a refreshing flavor with a little kick.

Serves 6-8

INGREDIENTS:

2 tbsp. mint leaves

6 to 8 whole cooked shrimps

2 cups cooked, peeled and chopped shrimp

2 cups full fat Greek yogurt

1 clove garlic

1 red chili

½ cup tomato juice, chilled

1¾ cups cucumber, diced

¼ cup cucumber for decoration

Ground black pepper

Salt

DIRECTIONS:

1. Place the diced cucumber in a food processor or blender and add the stock. Process to a fine puree.

2. Pour your mixture into a large bowl and add in the garlic, chili and tomato juice while stirring constantly.

3. Add the chopped shrimp, pepper, salt, yogurt and mint to taste.

4. Cover and chill for a couple of hours.

Before serving, decorate the soup with the whole shrimps and the remaining cucumber, thinly sliced into 12 to 16 pieces.

SUMMERTIME SOUP

A hot or cold summertime soup with the tang of crème fraîche!

Serves 4

INGREDIENTS:

2 pints beef broth

4 ounces fresh parsley

4 ounces sorrel leaves

3½ ounces crème fraîche

1 large egg, yolk only

¼ cup olive oil

DIRECTIONS:

1. Wash the parsley and the sorrel under plenty of cold water, drain.

2. Cut the sorrel into long strips and roughly chop the parsley.

3. Put the broth into a large saucepan and bring to a boil over a medium heat.

4. Add the sorrel and parsley and simmer together for a few minutes. Remove from the heat and set aside.

5. Strain about 1½ cups of liquid off the soup and place in a small pan. Allow to cool.

6. Mix the egg yolk with the crème fraîche in a small bowl. Beat in the oil.

7. Add this to the separated soup liquid by whisking it in carefully. You do not want the egg to cook.

8. Add this creamy mixture back into the main soup pot and serve immediately.

9. If cooled do not reheat.

THAI CHILI SOUP

This is a simple soup full of tasty herbs and spices. Infuse a Thai style into your cooking!

Serves 3

INGREDIENTS:

1 cup mushrooms, quartered

1 pack of firm plain tofu, drained, cut into small cubes

3 cups gluten-free chicken stock

2 cups coconut milk

2 tbsp. gluten-free soy sauce

4 stalks lemongrass (cut into 2 pieces after bruised)

4 tbsp. finely chopped cilantro

3 tbsp. lime juice

¼ tsp. ground black pepper

3 to 4 large chilies cut into chunks

1 tsp. erythritol

1 medium onion

3 to 4 kaffir lime leaves, torn

3 pieces galangal

DIRECTIONS:

1. Place the stock in a large pot, bring to a boil and add lemon grass, kaffir lime, onion, erythritol and galangal.

2. Bring to a boil and simmer for 5 minutes.

3. Put in the soy sauce, chilies and coconut milk. Let simmer again for 5 minutes.

4. Add the mushrooms and tofu.

5. When heated through remove from the heat.

6.   Add the lime juice and cilantro.

7. Serve in a large bowl.

APPETIZERS

A barbeque treat, but they can also be grilled inside for year round enjoyment. Marinated pork grilling outside in the fresh air! A smell sensation!

Serves 12

INGREDIENTS:

3 pounds boneless pork loin or fillet

2 green crunchy apples

6 large shallots

2 medium oranges

4 tablespoons olive oil

½ cup balsamic vinegar

6 cloves garlic

Salt and freshly ground black pepper

12 wooden skewers

DIRECTIONS:

1. Trim and cut the pork into 1 inch cubes.

2. Quarter, core and chop the apple into cubes of a similar size.

3. Cut the shallots into quarters.

4. Peel and crush the garlic.

5. Squeeze the juice from the oranges.

6. In a glass or ceramic bowl combine the orange juice, olive oil, vinegar and garlic. Season with salt and pepper.

7. Add the pork cubes to the marinade.

8. Cover the bowl and place in the fridge for about 2 hours.

9.   Whilst the pork is marinating start up the barbeque and prepare to a medium high heat.

10. Remove the pork from the fridge and thread the pieces onto the wooden skewers alternating with the apple pieces and the shallots.

11. Cook over the barbeque, turning carefully until cooked. Baste with the extra marinade.

12. Enjoy with a crispy green salad.

ASPARAGUS IN A PROSCIUTTO BLANKET

Scrumptious, quick and just so simple!

Serves 2 generously

INGREDIENTS:

16 spears of fresh green asparagus

8 slices prosciutto ham

Olive oil

DIRECTIONS:

1. Thoroughly wash and dry the asparagus spears and snap off the root end if tough.

2. Cut the ham slices in half and wrap each around an asparagus spear. Make sure that the base is covered – the top may be left open.

3. In a large skillet heat a little olive oil and fry the wrapped asparagus for about 6 minutes turning carefully half way through.

4. Serve whilst still hot for whichever meal you prefer.

Breakfast, lunch or for dinner? You decide! Maybe all three as these are so tasty.

BABA GHANOUSH – EGGPLANT SAVORY DIP

You must try this, especially for your veggie friends and family!

Serves 4

INGREDIENTS:

1 large eggplant

1 garlic clove

1 tablespoon fresh lime juice

1 tablespoon Tahini

1½ teaspoons olive oil

½ teaspoon cumin powder

Salt and freshly ground black pepper to taste

DIRECTIONS:

1. Cook the eggplant by pricking the skin all over and placing it in a hot oven for about 40 minutes.

2. Cool in a bowl of cold water and using the tip of a knife remove the skin and discard.

3. Place the eggplant in a blender or processor together with the rest of the ingredients and blend until smooth.

4. Adjust the seasoning to taste.

5. Cool completely and serve in a small bowl with a drizzle of olive oil on the top.

This garlicky dip will become one of your favorites!

BEEFY SCOTCH EGGS

Fancy a Scotch egg with a garlicky beefy coating? These will make your mouth water!

Serves 6

INGREDIENTS:

1¾ pounds minced beef (not too lean)

6 large eggs

10 medium cloves of garlic (more or less to taste)
paprika powder

DIRECTIONS:

1. Hard boil the eggs and when cool carefully take off the shell.

2. Crush or very finely chop the garlic.

3. Mix the mince and garlic and divide it into 6 equal portions

4. Flatten each portion of beef with your hands to form a flat, thin patty.

5. Mould each meat portion around an egg , gently forming it into a nicely rounded shape

6. Grill or bake the 'eggs' until cooked. (If you microwave them – be careful that the eggs do not explode!)

7. Serve the eggs cut in halves and sprinkled with paprika.

Filling and completely delicious! Make sure you share them!

BUTTERY CAULIFLOWER 'POPCORN'

You will have to taste this to believe how delicious it is!

Serves 6

INGREDIENTS:

1 large head of fresh cauliflower

6 tablespoons of olive oil

Salt to taste

DIRECTIONS:

1. Trim the cauliflower by discarding the core, outer leaves and extra thick stems.

2. Cut the florets into pieces about the size of a golf ball.

3. Wash carefully and drain thoroughly – the cauliflower must be dry.

4. Pre-heat the oven to 425°F and place the oven rack in the middle of the oven.

5. In a large bowl mix the olive oil and salt by whisking together.

6. Place the cauliflower pieces into the oil mixture and coat well, using your hands or a wooden spoon.

7. Spread the coated cauliflower pieces on a baking sheet.

8. Place in the oven and roast for about 60 minutes turning every 15 minutes or so to ensure each piece is evenly caramelized.

9. When a beautiful, golden brown color, remove from the oven.

10. Serve whilst still warm.

Sweet, crunchy cauliflower at its best!

CHICKEN AND BACON POPPERS

OMG! What is that delicious smell emanating from the kitchen?

Makes 30

INGREDIENTS:

1¼ pounds of chicken fillets

10 rashers of bacon

DIRECTIONS:

1. Pre-heat the oven to 375°F

2. Prepare a baking tray by covering it with foil.

3. Cut the chicken fillet into 30 even sized pieces.

4. Cut each bacon rasher into 3.

5. Wrap a piece of bacon around each piece of chicken.

6. Place the chicken wraps onto the foil lined tray with the bacon seam down.

7. Place the tray on the middle rack of the oven and bake for about 25 minutes until brown and the bacon is crisp. You can turn the poppers half way through if you like.

8. Remove from the oven and drain the excess fat away on a paper towel.

9. Place a cocktail stick in each popper and serve hot.

Your guests will love these drool worthy treats!

CHICKEN WINGS WITH A ZING

Want to get that barbeque off to a swinging start? Try these tasty snacks to serve before the mains for a finger-licking taste sensation! Maybe you should make a double quantity!

Serves 8 –10

INGREDIENTS:

1 small onion roughly chopped

2 hot red peppers (or to taste) - seeds removed

4 peeled garlic cloves

½ cup cilantro or basil (packed down)

2 limes - zested

¼ cup lime juice

2 tablespoons extra-virgin fish sauce

2 tablespoons coconut aminos (soy-free seasoning sauce)

Freshly ground pepper

6 pounds chicken wings

2 tablespoons melted butter or olive oil

4 wedged limes to serve

DIRECTIONS:

1. In a food processor or blender, blend all the ingredients together except for the chicken, melted fat and lime wedges, until a smooth puree.

2. In a large marinading dish or bowl (not aluminium due to the acid content) add the marinade to the prepared chicken wings and mix well to cover the wings.

3. Leave the chicken in the fridge for at least half an hour but not more than 8 hours.

4. Remove the wings from the fridge 30 minutes before you cook

them to bring them to room temperature.

5. Prepare a medium heat barbeque and grease the grid with the melted fat or oil (Use a wad of paper towel to do this and be careful as the grid will be hot!)

6. Grill the wings turning once during cooking; making sure that the skin becomes crispy and golden brown.

7. If it is a cold and rainy day these zingy wings may also be cooked in your oven. Pre-heat your oven to 375°F (Convection) or 400°F (Regular setting).

8. Line a baking tray with foil and place the wings on a greased wire rack in the tray.

9. Bake them for about 30 minutes, turning carefully about halfway through.

10. Serve with lime wedges (and paper napkins) and Enjoy!

The aroma will be amazing but you will have to wait about 15 to 20 minutes for the wings to be cooked through on the barbeque and a bit longer in the oven! It is worth the wait!

CAULIFLOWER MAC AND CHEESE NUGGETS

Cauliflower takes on a different guise in these cheesy nuggets. Serve them with slices of avocado and some crispy watercress.

Serves 6

INGREDIENTS:

1 large head cauliflower, broken into florets

6 ounces Monterey Jack cheese

1 tsp. powdered garlic

1 tsp. powdered onion

3 medium fresh eggs, beaten

1 large fresh egg

¼ cup (59ml) unsweetened almond milk

1 cup (70g) coarsely crushed pork rinds

Salt and freshly ground black pepper to season

DIRECTIONS:

1. Cook the cauliflower in some salted water until tender – do not let it become mushy.

2. Drain very well. Pat dry with a paper towel and spread out on an open plate for 30 minutes to finish drying.

3. Pre-heat the oven to 375°F.

4. Prepare a baking sheet by covering it with parchment paper.

5. Place the dry cauliflower in a processor and pulse until it looks like breadcrumbs.

6. Place the cauliflower in a large bowl and stir in the cheese, garlic and onion powder and seasoning to taste.

7. Stir in the beaten eggs, using enough to give a stiff mixture.

8. Beat the large egg and milk together in a shallow bowl.

9.   Place the pork rinds on a plate.

10. Divide the cauliflower mixture into 12 serves and form small nuggets with damp hands.

11. Place each nugget in the egg mixture and roll in the pork rinds.

12. Carefully place on the prepared baking sheet.

13. Bake for 20 – 25 minutes in the hot oven until nicely golden and crisp.

14. Serve hot.

CRISPY BRUSSEL SPROUTS CRUNCH

Simply delicious and irresistibly good!

Serves 3

INGREDIENTS:

About 2 pounds of green or purple brussel sprouts

2 tablespoons of butter, bacon fat or ghee

Salt to taste

Lemon zest and cracked black pepper

DIRECTIONS:

1. Preheat oven to 350°F.

2. Remove enough large outer leaves of the sprouts to fill 2 cups

3. Combine gently, the leaves, butter, bacon fat or ghee, and salt in a bowl.

4. Divide the leaves in a single layer on each of two large baking trays that have been lined with parchment or greaseproof paper

5. Bake for about 10 minutes until crisp and beginning to brown around the edges.

6. Sprinkle with some lemon zest and pepper

7. Eat while still crisp and crunchy.

Maybe you should make extra in anticipation of the demand?

CRISPY KALE

Another fabulous, tasty vegetable crisp recipe for you to try! A quick and tasty snack!

Makes a large bowlful

INGREDIENTS:

A large bunch of fresh kale

2 tablespoons coconut oil

Salt to taste

DIRECTIONS:

1. Pre-heat the oven to 325°F.

2. Carefully wash the kale leaves in plenty of running water to remove any grit.

3. Dry well.

4. Remove the tough stems and tear the remaining leaves into smallish pieces of about 1½ inches. They do not have to be the same shapes so don't use a pair of scissors for this! You will need about 8 cups of leaves.

5. Place the torn pieces into a large bowl and pour over the coconut oil which has been warmed to make it less viscous.

6. Toss the leaves around to ensure that they are evenly covered with oil

7. Spread the leaves out on one or two large baking sheets and sprinkle with a little salt.

8. Bake for about 25 minutes until the leaves are crisp.

9. Eat whilst still warm.

Store these delicious chips when they are cold in an airtight container – they will be just as good the next day!

DEVILLED EGGS A'LA GUACAMOLE

A pleasingly, tangy, version of Eggs a'la Guacamole.

Makes 16 halves

INGREDIENTS:

8 large fresh eggs

2 ripe avocado pears

1 tablespoon hot chilli sauce

1 teaspoons of lime juice

Pinch of celery salt

Freshly ground black pepper

DIRECTIONS:

1. Hard boil the eggs and when they are cool peel them.

2. Cut the eggs in half lengthways

3. Remove the egg yolks and place in a medium sized bowl.

4. Peel and pit the avocado pears and place the flesh in the same bowl as the egg yolks.

5. Add the lime juice and the hot sauce together with a good pinch of celery salt.

6. Mash together well, with a fork, and crack in some black pepper to taste.

7. Using a teaspoon, refill the egg whites with the avocado mixture.

8. Arrange on a serving plate and enjoy.

An up to date and healthy version of stuffed eggs! A firm favorite!

GOLDEN CHICKEN BITES

Chicken Nuggets with crispy coconut – you must try these!

Serves 6

INGREDIENTS:

1½ pounds of freshly ground chicken

2 egg yolks

1½ teaspoons onion flakes

½ teaspoon garlic flakes

½ teaspoon paprika powder

Large pinch salt

¼ teaspoon cracked black pepper

¾ cup of almond flour/ground almonds plus another ½ cup for coating

¾ cup unsweetened shredded coconut

¾ cup coconut oil

Salt and pepper to taste for coating

DIRECTIONS:

1. Preheat the oven to 375°F.

2. In a large bowl combine the ground chicken, ¾ cup of almond flour, seasonings and the egg yolks. Mix well.

3. In a separate bowl combine the ½ cup almond flour, the shredded coconut and salt and pepper to taste.

4. Form the chicken mixture into small balls with wet hands to stop it sticking and roll each as it is made in the coating mixture. You should have about 24 chicken bites.

5. Heat the oil in a skillet and gently fry the bites for about 4 minutes.

6. Drain bites and place on a baking sheet covered with

parchment paper. Finish cooking in the pre-heated oven for another 5 minutes or so.

7. Cool and serve with a sauce of your choice.

Delish served with the barbeque sauce recipe. These taste like the REAL thing!

GREEN SCRAMBLED EGGS

Food for Dr. Seuss maybe? Maybe, but try this without the ham – great fun!

Serves 4

INGREDIENTS:

8 large fresh farm eggs

8 large kale leaves – washed but left whole

Large pinch of salt

Olive oil

DIRECTIONS:

1. Crack the eggs into a blender or food processor together with the kale leaves and a pinch of salt to taste.

2. Blend or process until smooth.

3. Heat the oil in skillet over a medium heat

4. When the oil is hot, pour in the egg mixture.

5. Leave for a moment and then stir until scrambled to your preference.

6. Serve hot with bacon or accompaniments of your choice.

These eggs I love! I love them yes, these bright green eggs I love the best!

GROUND BEEF JERKY

A fabulous jerky recipe that can be dried in a conventional oven!

Makes 40 small pieces

INGREDIENTS:

3 pounds ground beef

3 tablespoons salt

4 tablespoons coconut aminos

Olive oil

DIRECTIONS:

1. Mix the salt into the beef in a large bowl.

2. Oil the base of two large deep baking sheets with olive oil.

3. Press the beef into the sheets dividing it evenly between the two. It should not be more that ¼ inch thick.

4. Brush the beef with the Coconut aminos before placing in a low oven 150°F.

5. Leave to dry out overnight, or for about 10 hours, until the jerky is hard.

6. Pour off any fat that may have accumulated.

7. Turn out and cool. Break into manageable sized pieces.

8. Store in an airtight container in the fridge.

Munch away!

GUACAMOLE AND VEGETABLE DUNK

Versatile guacamole comes to the rescue for a quick and easy party dip.

Makes 1 snack plate

INGREDIENTS:

1 quantity of guacamole

1 red bell pepper

1 yellow bell pepper

2 small carrots

1 small cucumber

1 small cauliflower

DIRECTIONS:

1. Place the guacamole in a dip bowl and place it in the centre of a large plate.

2. Wash, peel, seed and cut up the vegetables into finger sized portions.

3. Arrange decoratively on the plate around the guacamole bowl.

4. Serve and enjoy.

Delicious and yes, it is healthy!

HERBY CRACKERS

The guacamole needs some crackers please!

Makes about 24

INGREDIENTS:

2 cups almond flour

1/2 teaspoon sea salt

2 tablespoon dried mixed Italian herbs

2 tablespoons cold water

1 large egg white

1 tablespoon olive oil

DIRECTIONS:

1. Pre-heat the oven to 350°F.

2. In a small bowl mix the flour, herbs and salt together so that they are well combined.

3. In another bowl beat together the egg, water and olive oil.

4. Add the egg mixture to the flour and stir until you get a stiff dough. Knead a little with your hands if necessary to bring all of the ingredients together.

5. Cover a board with parchment paper and place the dough on it. Flatten with the ball of your hand.

6. Place another piece of parchment on top and roll out evenly to about 1/8 inch thick.

7. Try and roll out the dough to a rectangular shape to fit onto a baking tray. Don't worry if you have a few raggedy bits – they will be great tasters!

8. Transfer the bottom parchment onto a baking tray. Use a sharp knife to cut into cracker sixed shapes.

9. Bake in the centre of the oven for 10 minutes.

10. Turn off the oven and leave the crackers in for another 10 minutes or so to get nice and crispy golden brown.

11. Remove from the oven and tray and cool.

Crunchy and delicious! Great with a savory dip for a pre-dinner or party snack!

JAPANESE FRIED PEPPERS

A sweet, salty and spicy appetizer!

Serves 4

INGREDIENTS:

20 Japanese shishito peppers (Sweet, slightly hot peppers)

4 teaspoons of olive oil

2 cloves of freshly minced garlic

2 small juicy limes

Sea salt to taste

DIRECTIONS:

1.   Heat the olive oil in a skillet until very hot.

2.   Add the peppers to the oil and stir fry until they take on a slightly charred look and become wrinkled. About 8 minutes.

3.   Add the garlic to the pan making sure that it does not burn. Stir around gently for about another minute.

4.   Remove the peppers from the pan and squeeze over some lime juice. Sprinkle with salt to taste.

5.   Serve whilst still hot.

Hot and spicy! Maybe only for the brave!

LIP SMACKING MUSHROOM CHIPS

Ever craved for that elusive umami flavor? This could be where you find it!

Serves 4

INGREDIENTS:

1¼ pounds large oyster mushrooms

4 tablespoon melted butter

Sea salt

Freshly ground black pepper to taste

DIRECTIONS:

1. Pre-heat the oven before you start to 300°F.

2. Line a few cookie trays with baking parchment.

3. Clean the mushrooms.

4. Cut the mushrooms in half lengthwise and slice thinly.

5. Dry the mushrooms slices thoroughly by gently patting them with paper towel.

6. Brush melted butter on both sides of the slices, and season with salt and pepper to taste.

7. Arrange the slices, with spaces in between, as a single layer on the prepared cookie trays.

8. Place in trays in the oven and bake for about 40 until the mushrooms are golden brown and crispy. This is very important!

9. Repeat with any slices you may have left over that did not fit onto the trays first time around.

Mouthwatering mushroomy morsels... Mmmmm....

PECAN NUT MUNCHIES

A great source of energy for that monster workout! These munchies are great for breakfast, lunch boxes or whenever you fancy a treat.

Makes 6

INGREDIENTS:

3 ounces chocolate low carb protein powder (gluten free)

1 tablespoon ground cinnamon

½ cup chopped pecan nuts

2 tablespoons ground flax seed

2 tablespoons almond butter (or other nut butter)

1 tablespoon non-dairy brownie mix

½ cup unsweetened almond milk

DIRECTIONS:

1. Place all of the ingredients into a large bowl and mix well with a wooden spoon until a thick paste is formed.

2. Divide into six fairly even portions and form into bars.

3. Place the bars in the fridge to harden for a couple of hours.

4. Pre-heat the oven to very hot 400 °F.

5. Place the bars on a foil lined baking sheet and bake for 10 – 12 minutes. Make sure that they do not burn.

6. Remove from the oven and cool.

7. Serve.

SALTY SESAME CRACKER BISCUITS

Fancy something savory with a dip or a piece of cheese? These are indeed your answer! Serve at your next get together and watch the smiles of satisfaction from your guests!

Makes 48 small crackers

INGREDIENTS:

1½ cups almond flour

¾ teaspoons sea salt

½ cup toasted sesame seeds

1 egg

1 tablespoon olive oil

DIRECTIONS:

1. Pre-heat the oven to 350°F

2. In a large bowl mix together the almond flour, salt and sesame seeds.

3. Whisk the egg and oil together in a small bowl.

4. Stir the egg mixture into the dry ingredients and mix well to form a dough.

5. Roll out the dough between 2 sheets of parchment paper until it is very thin and fits a baking sheet in area.

6. Don't worry if it is not perfect! The crackers will taste amazing whatever their shape!

7. Remove the top piece of paper and place the bottom one with the dough on the baking sheet.

8. Cut with a sharp knife into 2 inch squares or diamonds or rectangles – whatever takes your fancy!

9. Bake for about 10 minutes until your crackers are a lovely golden color.

10. Remove from the oven and cool just a little before breaking the crackers apart and cooling on a wire rack.

SHRIMP SNACK

Delicious for a quick lunch, with a crispy green side salad!

Serves 4

INGREDIENTS:

1 pound raw shrimp

4 tablespoons olive oil

1 tablespoon chilli powder

1 tablespoon garlic powder

1 tablespoon finely chopped parsley

Salt and freshly ground black pepper to taste

DIRECTIONS:

1. Clean, peel and de-vein the shrimp.

2. Place a skillet on the stove top and heat over a medium high heat.

3. Add the olive oil to the pan.

4. When the oil is hot, quickly stir fry the shrimp for a minute or so.

5. Add the chilli, garlic and parsley to the pan and mix gently into the shrimp.

6. Fry for another 4 minutes until the shrimp turns pink and is fully cooked.

Serve as a pre-dinner snack too! You just need a few tooth picks and some table napkins to soak up the really lip smacking juices!

SPICY ASSORTED NUTS

Mix it up! Use an assortment of nuts as in the recipe or just choose your absolute favorites! Same recipe for all!

Makes a medium bowl full

INGREDIENTS:

2 teaspoons almond oil

1 pound mixed raw nuts

2 teaspoons chilli pepper

1 teaspoon allspice powder

4 teaspoon finely chopped fresh parsley

DIRECTIONS:

1. Pre-heat the oven to 350°F.

2. Prepare a baking sheet with parchment paper.

3. Mix all of the ingredients together except for the parsley.

4. Place on the baking sheet.

5. Roast for 10 minutes, turning half way through so as the nuts are evenly coated and evenly roasted.

6. Make sure that the nuts do not burn.

7. Remove from the oven and toss in the chopped parsley.

Nuts have never tasted like such toasty goodness before!

SPICY CHICKEN SKEWERS

Use low carb. sweet chili sauce to baste these spicy chicken sticks for a great start to any meal.

Serves 6

INGREDIENTS:

2 pounds chicken breast meat, cubed

½ cup olive oil

7 cloves garlic, finely chopped

½ cup cilantro, chopped

2 tbsp. white vinegar

1 large red chili (to taste), finely chopped

3 tbsp. powdered sugar substitute

Salt and pepper to season

DIRECTIONS:

1. In a small bowl mix together the oil, 6 of the garlic cloves and the cilantro.

2. Season with salt and pepper.

3. Place the chicken cubes in a large bowl and cover them with the cilantro marinade. Ensure they are well covered. Use your hands if necessary.

4. Cover and place in the refrigerator for several hours or even overnight.

5. While the chicken is marinating, make the sweet chili sauce.

6. In a small saucepan heat together the vinegar and sugar substitute. Add the extra clove of garlic and the chili pepper.

7. Simmer gently for a couple of minutes.

8. Pour into a small bowl to cool.

9. When you are ready to cook the chicken pre-heat a griddle to medium.

10. Thread the chicken onto skewers and place on the hot griddle and cook, turning frequently for 10 – 15 minutes until cooked through.

11. As the Skewers are cooking baste them with the chili sauce.

12. Be careful they do not burn but only turn a glazed golden brown.

13. Remove from the heat and serve while still hot.

VANILLA AND ALMOND BARS

A handy bar to have in the fridge! Grab and Go! Enjoy as a breakfast treat or whenever you feel like an energy pick-me-up.

Makes 4

INGREDIENTS:

4 ounces vanilla low carb protein powder (gluten free)

4 tablespoons almond butter

4 tablespoons ground flaxseed

½ cup water

DIRECTIONS:

1. In a medium sized bowl place the protein and the almond butter and mix to a smooth paste.

2. In a separate bowl mix the ground flax seed and the water.

3. Add the water and flaxseed mixture to the protein and butter and combine well together to form a thick paste.

4. Divide the mixture into four and mold carefully into a bar shape.

5. Wrap each bar in tin foil and place in the fridge to harden.

Leave for at least 8 hours or overnight.

WOW FACTOR PUMPKIN SEEDS

Dip into your pocket for a handful of these tasty seeds whilst you are on the run!

About 3 cups of seeds

INGREDIENTS:

3 cups of raw pumpkin seeds – rinsed and dried if taken directly from a pumpkin

2 tablespoons coconut oil

1 tablespoon chilli or peri peri powder

Sea salt to taste

Cayenne pepper to sprinkle

DIRECTIONS:

1. Pre-heat the oven to 350°F

2. In a large bowl place all of the ingredients except the cayenne pepper.

3. Toss well together and spread on a baking sheet.

4. Bake for about 12 minutes, turning the mixture half way through to allow for even browning.

5. Cool, sprinkle with extra cayenne and tuck in.

If these last until the end of the day you make them store the leftovers in an airtight container in the fridge. They only last a week but they will likely be finished long before then!

ZESTY SHRIMP COCKTAIL

Maybe this one will transport you back in time to the 1970's? A bang up to date version!

Serves 6

INGREDIENTS:

1½ pounds of shrimp

1 6 ounce can of tomato puree

¼ cup tomato juice

1 tablespoon horseradish sauce

1 tablespoon lime juice

½ teaspoon chilli sauce

Salt to taste

DIRECTIONS:

1. Clean, peel and de-vein the shrimp leaving the tails on.

2. Cook in the shrimp in gently boiling salted water until the turn pink and are cooked.

3. Take the shrimp out of the water and cool.

4. Combine the tomato puree, tomato juice, horseradish, lime juice and chilli in a bowl.

5. Taste and add salt it needed.

6. Cover the sauce and leave for the flavors to develop whilst the shrimps are cooling.

7. Place the sauce in a bowl in the centre of a plate and surround it with the cooked shrimp.

8. Using the tails to hold the shrimp, dunk and enjoy.

Wow! Now that really gets the taste buds a' tinglin!

DINNER

ALMOND AND FLAXSEED BURGERS

A raw burger, which is very filling! Serve with salad on the side. Add extra garlic if you like the taste.

Serves 4

INGREDIENTS:

2 cup raw almonds

1 cup ground flaxseed

2 cloves garlic

4 tablespoons balsamic vinegar

4 tablespoons olive oil

Sea salt

DIRECTIONS:

1. Place all of the ingredients into a blender and pulse until well blended. Add salt to taste.

2. Form into 4 patties.

ASPARAGUS AND WHITE BEAN PASTA

Slightly crunchy asparagus paired with white beans make for a filling and refreshing entrée!

Serves 4

INGREDIENTS:

2 pounds wheat free penne pasta

1 can white beans, drained and rinsed

1 bunch asparagus, cut into 1-inch pieces

8 baby Portobello mushrooms, halved

½ red onion, wedged thinly

4 cloves garlic, minced

½ cup fresh basil, finely chopped

1 tbsp. nutritional yeast

1 tbsp. balsamic vinegar

3 tbsp. olive oil

1 pinch salt ground black pepper to taste

½ cup sun dried tomatoes, chopped

DIRECTIONS:

1. Fill a medium saucepan with water, and bring to the boil. Once it is boiling, add the pasta and season with salt.
2. Heat a frying pan or a wok, and pour in 1 tbsp. of olive oil.
3. Add the asparagus, mushrooms, red onion, and garlic, and mix well.
4. Add 2 tbsp. of water to steam. Cover the pan with a lid and frequently stir the mixture for about 7-8 minutes or until the vegetables are tender.

5. Transfer the pasta into a medium-large pan, and mix in the vegetables.

6. Add balsamic vinegar and the white beans. Stir it well until the pasta is well coated.

7. Combine 2 tbsp. of olive oil in another bowl, together the yeast, and fresh basil to create a paste. Add the paste to the pasta and stir well to coat.

8. Garnish with a cupful of sun dried tomatoes.

9. Serve warm.

BEEF STEAK AND MUSHROOMS

This steak is delicious and it just takes a few moments to make. Use a stronger cheese if you wish and leave the steaks whole for a bigger portion!

Serves 4

INGREDIENTS:

4 x 6 ounce beef steaks

1 cup onion, sliced

2 green bell peppers, sliced

8 ounces mushrooms, sliced

¼ cup olive oil

Butter to fry with

2 ounce mild white cheese, sliced

Salt and pepper

DIRECTIONS:

1. Season and grill the steaks as you would like them.

2. Cut into bite sized pieces and place in a heatproof dish.

3. Sauté the onion, mushrooms and pepper in a little butter and the olive oil until caramelized.

4. Season to taste and spoon over the steak.

5. Layer the cheese slices on top and melt under a broiler until brown and bubbly.

BISON BOLOGNAISE

A wonderful way to celebrate a healthy and adventurous life is by combining pasta with sultry, bison meat. Your diet will not be the same again, a better comfort with a simple taste.

Serves 4-6

INGREDIENTS:

1 pound fresh ground beef

1 pound wheat free tagliatelle or spaghetti

1 onion, chopped

1 clove garlic, minced

1 tbsp. Tomato paste

2 15 ounce cans tomatoes, chopped

8-10 button mushrooms, sliced

1 whole red bell pepper, chopped

1 whole green bell pepper, chopped

2 tsp. Mixed herbs, dried

1 tsp. Freshly ground black pepper

1 tbsp. Balsamic vinegar

1 tbsp. Olive oil

Parmesan cheese, grated

DIRECTIONS:

1. Heat a large saucepan, and then pour in the olive oil. Sauté the chopped onion until translucent.

2. Add the ground bison and cook until browned. Strain off any excess juices.

3. Combine with peppers, mushrooms, mixed herbs, and season with black pepper. Add to the bison mince.

4. Heat and simmer, stirring occasionally for 43-45 minutes. A few minutes before the mixture is ready, mix in the balsamic vinegar.

5. Boil some water in another pan and add the pasta noodles. Season with salt, and boil for about 3 minutes. Keep the pasta warm over a low heat.

6. Transfer the pasta into a serving dish and pour over the sauce, mix until equally distributed.

7. Serve hot with red wine. Sprinkle some Parmesan cheese over the top if desired.

CHICKEN TIKKA MASALA

This one will tickle your taste buds and satisfy your curry craving!

Serves 4

INGREDIENTS:

2 inches ginger root, finely grated

7 cloves garlic

¾ cup full fat Greek yogurt

1 tbsp. lime juice

1 tbsp. cilantro leaves, chopped

1½ tsp. chili powder

1 tsp. ground turmeric

1 large pinch garam masala

1 pinch salt

4 large chicken breasts, skinless and chopped into pieces

2 tbsp. olive oil

1 large red onion, chopped

1 tsp. ground coriander

1 cup chopped tomatoes

1 red bell pepper, chopped

DIRECTIONS:

1. Combine half of the ginger, 3 crushed cloves garlic, yogurt, lime juice, cilantro, half of the chili powder and turmeric, gram masala and a pinch of salt in a small bowl for the marinade.

2. Mix well and leave for 15 minutes for the flavors to combine.

3. Place the chicken pieces into the ready-made marinade.

4. Rub generously to evenly coat the chicken, and leave to rest for an hour for the flavors to infuse.

5. Heat the oil in a large skillet and sauté the onion until soft and translucent.

6. Add the rest of the garlic and ginger and stir fry for a couple of minutes.

7. Stir in the rest of the spices and mix well.

8. Add the chopped tomatoes and peppers and sauté for a few minutes more.

9. Remove ½ cup of mixture and purée. Return to the skillet.

10. Remove the chicken pieces from the marinade – do not take the marinade off and add to the tomato mixture.

11. Mix well and cover with a lid. Bring to the boil and then simmer for about 30 minutes. Adjust seasoning.

12. Serve.

CLAM PASTA

A quick and easy way to enjoy a hard days work is with the succulent and unique taste of the sea. One of the least used shellfish is a great addition into this pasta.

2 Servings

INGREDIENTS:

7 ounces canned clams

1 onion, finely chopped

4 ounces wheat free spaghetti

7 ounces canned tomatoes, chopped

1 tbsp. Tomato purée

½ red bell pepper, chopped

½ bell green pepper, chopped

1 clove garlic, crushed

3 dashes chili sauce

1 tbsp. Olive oil

1 pinch ground black pepper

DIRECTIONS:

1. Heat a saucepan and pour in the olive oil. Add the garlic and onion and fry until brown.

2. Mix the tomato purée, chopped tomatoes, peppers and chilli sauce.

3. Bring to the boil, then lower the heat and simmer for about 10 minutes.

4. Pour in the clams and season with black pepper. Cook for 4 – 5 minutes.

5. Boil some water; add the salt and the spaghetti. Boil until al dente.

6. Drain the spaghetti, put it on a serving plate and add the sauce.

7. Serve hot.

CREAMY CHICKEN WITH MUSHROOMS

Chicken smothered in mushrooms, an all-time favorite in warming, elegant food.

Serves 8

INGREDIENTS:

2 pounds chicken breast, skinned and boned

6 tbsp. butter

2 cups chicken broth

1 medium carrot, peeled and diced

2 stalks celery, washed and finely sliced

1 medium shallot, diced

1 small red bell pepper, seeded and finely diced

1 small red chili, seeded and finely chopped

12 ounces fresh button mushrooms, quartered

1½ cups heavy cream

2 tsp. xanthan gum

½ tbsp. fresh parsley, chopped

Salt and pepper to season

DIRECTIONS:

1. Melt 2 tbsp. butter in a large skillet (with lid) over a medium high heat.

2. Add the chicken breast and sauté until brown on all sides.

3. Pour over 1 cup of chicken broth and cover the skillet.

4. Reduce the heat to a simmer and cook for 15 – 20 minutes until cooked through. Cook for a little longer if necessary.

5. Remove the chicken from the skillet and set aside.

6. Pour off the cooking liquid and set aside.

7. When the chicken is cool, chop into bite sized pieces.

8. Place the rest of the butter in a large clean skillet and heat over a medium high heat.

9. Sauté the carrot, celery, shallot and red bell pepper and the chili until tender.

10. Add the mushrooms and continue to sauté until the mushrooms turn a golden brown.

11. Stir in the remaining broth, the cooking liquid from the chicken and the cream.

12. Bring up to the boil and stir in the xanthan gum.

13. Season to taste with salt and pepper.

14. Stir in the cooked chicken and allow the dish to heat through completely before serve.

15. Serve sprinkled with chopped parsley.

GARLIC PORK CHOPS

These chops have a tasty butter sauce which can be used over other grilled meats if you wish to make some changes to your diet.

Serves 4

INGREDIENTS:

2 ounces butter, melted

1 small onion, chopped

3 cloves garlic, finely chopped

½ cup fresh parsley, chopped

2 tbsp. olive oil

4 thick loin pork chops

Salt and pepper

DIRECTIONS:

1. Heat the oil and butter in a large skillet.
2. Sprinkle the chops with seasoning and brown in the skillet.
3. Set the chops aside, keep warm.
4. In the same skillet fry the onions and garlic until the onion is tender.
5. Add the parsley, stirring well.
6. Place the chops back into the skillet and cover with a lid.
7. Turn the heat to low and simmer for 10 minutes to warm through.
8. Serve with green vegetables.

GRILLED TROUT WITH SHRIMP AND HORSERADISH

Even if you didn't spend all day waiting with your fishing pole to catch your trout, it will taste just as good with a touch of horseradish.

Makes about 24

INGREDIENTS:

2 whole trout, cleaned and dried, heads removed

10 tiger prawns, with shells intact

1 tbsp. Natural horseradish sauce

1 tbsp. Balsamic vinegar

1 tbsp. Olive oil

1 pinch ground black pepper

DIRECTIONS:

1. Combine the balsamic vinegar, olive oil, and season with fresh ground black pepper in a small bowl. Stir it well.

2. With a sharp knife slash the sides of the trout.

3. Brush the mix evenly on the trout, pouring generously on the cut sides.

4. Prepare grilling equipment and place the sauced trout to grill.

5. Grill the trout for about 8-10 minutes. Repeat the brushing of the sauce until cooked well.

6. Dip the prawns in the remaining sauce mixture.

7. Heat a pan, place the sauced prawns in it and cook until tender or pink.

8. Brush the other side with the sauce mix, and cook again until tender or pink.

9. Put the cooked trout on a serving plate and garnish with prepared prawns, and horseradish sauce. Serve.

ITALIAN BOLOGNESE

A rich beef sauce to serve over spaghetti squash. Make a big batch as it freezes well and you will always have an extra meal on hand.

Serves 6

INGREDIENTS:

1½ pounds ground beef

4 ounces bacon, chopped

1 large onion, finely chopped

4 cloves garlic, finely chopped

2 tbsp. olive oil

2 tbsp. tomato paste

½ cup dry red wine

1 tsp. powdered paprika

1 tsp. powdered coriander

2 bay leaves

1 cup beef broth

Salt and pepper to season

Parmesan cheese to serve

DIRECTIONS:

1. Heat the oil in a large saucepan over a medium high heat.

2. Add the chopped onions and the garlic and sauté until the onions become translucent.

3. Add the bacon and fry until it begins to release its fat.

4. Add the ground beef and brown well, breaking up any pieces that may need it.

5. Add the rest of the ingredients except the cheese and mix well together.

6. Lower the heat and simmer for 1½ - 2 hours until rich and thick.

7. Serve hot with plenty of Parmesan cheese on top.

POT ROAST BEEF

This dish could also be made in a slow cooker, if you have one.

Serves 8

INGREDIENTS:

3 pounds beef, chuck or a round of beef

1 onion, coarsely chopped

1 head of garlic cut in half horizontally

6 rashers bacon, chopped

1 cup beef broth

2 tbsp. gluten-free Worcestershire sauce

3 tbsp. red wine vinegar

2 tsp. hot ready-made mustard

2 tbsp. erythritol

2 large sprigs fresh thyme

Salt and pepper to season

DIRECTIONS:

1. Pre-heat the oven to 350°F.

2. Heat a large skillet over a medium high heat and add the bacon.

3. Sauté the bacon until the fat begins to run and it is cooked but not crisp.

4. Add the onion and sauté until translucent. Set aside.

5. Season the beef with salt and pepper and brown it on all sides in the skillet.

6. Place the browned beef in a large casserole dish that has a lid.

7. Add the onions, bacon and the 2 pieces of garlic head.

8. Mix together the broth, Worcestershire sauce, vinegar, mustard and sugar substitute.

9. Pour this liquid over the beef. Add a sprig of thyme either side of the beef.

10. Cover the casserole dish with the lid and place in the hot oven.

11. Cook for 2½ – 3 hours until the meat is tender.

12. When cooked, lift the meat out of the juices and the casserole and place on a plate. Cover with foil and allow to rest for 15 minutes.

13. Skim off any extra fat in the casserole, remove the thyme and squeeze the garlic to remove the flesh from the skins.

14. Discard the thyme and garlic skins.

15. Reduce sauce if liked and serve in a separate dish.

16. Slice the meat and serve with green seasonal vegetables.

RATATOUILLE

Serve hot or cold as a salad, this versatile vegetable dish tastes delicious both ways!

Serves 8

INGREDIENTS:

½ cup olive oil

½ cup onion, chopped

16 ounces eggplant, cubed

1 large yellow bell pepper

8 ounces zucchini, chopped

4 cloves garlic, finely chopped

12 ounces tomatoes, skinned and chopped

¼ cup vegetable broth

Few drops chili sauce

½ cup fresh basil, torn

Salt and pepper to taste

DIRECTIONS:

1. Heat the olive oil in a skillet and fry the onion until it is sizzling.

2. Add the eggplant cubes and cook for about 5 minutes.

3. Sprinkle the onions and eggplant with salt.

4. Add the yellow pepper to the skillet and cook for a couple of minutes. Finely add the zucchini and cook through.

5. Add the garlic at this stage followed by the tomatoes.

6. Stir well before adding the broth.

7. Your dish is ready when the tomatoes collapse and the eggplant is very soft.

8. Season to taste and add the hot sauce.

9. Toss in the torn basil and serve.

ROASTED SWORDFISH WITH BASIL

Roasting the swordfish gives it a nice brown color and delicious flavor. Sprinkled with fresh basil for an extra taste sensation!

Serves 4

INGREDIENTS:

4 swordfish steaks

1 tbsp. olive oil

Salt and ground black pepper

1 cup lima beans, washed and drained

2 tbsp. chilli oil

1 large chilli, seeded and chopped

8 spring onions, trimmed and finely sliced

Fresh basil, shredded

1 large tomato, skinned, seeded and chopped

DIRECTIONS:

1. Preheat the oven at 400°F.

2. Brush oil on the swordfish and sprinkle with salt and pepper.

3. Place on a baking tray lined with parchment paper.

4. In a small pan cook the lima beans in the chili oil with the chili and spring onions for about 5 minutes.

5. Put the fish in the oven for about 10 minutes.

6. Add chopped tomato and chopped basil to the lima beans and simmer it for about 5 minutes. Season to taste.

7. Serve the fish on hot plates with the lima beans sprinkled on top. Use the remaining basil to decorate.

SPAGHETTI SQUASH

If you are looking for a unique twist on pasta, then you have found the right recipe. The spaghetti squash makes a great gluten-free alternative to typical wheat pasta.

Serves 6-8

INGREDIENTS:

2 tbsp. olive oil

1 small yellow onion, diced

6 cloves garlic, diced

6 baby carrots, diced

½ cup fresh basil, shredded

1 tsp. red pepper flakes

2 tsp. oregano

1 tsp. freshly ground black pepper

28 ounce tin whole tomatoes, crushed

2 tbsp. tomato paste

2 cups spinach

1 large spaghetti squash

2 tbsp. butter

¼ cup dry red wine

8 ounces mozzarella cheese, sliced

DIRECTIONS:

1. Pre-heat the oven to 350°F.

2. Heat a medium saucepan over medium heat and pour in the olive oil.

3. Add the onions and carrots. Sauté for 2-3 minutes, and then add the diced garlic.

4. Mix in the crushed tomatoes and red wine, and stir well.

5. Add the tomato paste, oregano, red pepper flakes, and season with ground pepper. Bring it to a boil.

6. Lower the heat and add the basil.

7. Slice the spaghetti squash in half and deseed.

8. Place 1 tbsp. of butter on each half. Cover with waxed paper and put it into a microwave for 8-10 minutes to break it apart.

9. Using a fork separate the squash into strands.

10. Add the spinach to the sauce mixture, and stir. Remove the sauce from heat.

11. Mix the spaghetti squash and sauce, pouring the sauce evenly over it.

12. Place the mixture in a baking dish. Put the mozzarella on top of the mixture. Bake for 45 minutes.

13. Serve hot on a serving plate.

SPICY CHILI PORK CHOPS

Yum! Juicy pork chops at their very best; heavenly with a green salad and an extra side of chopped avocado.

Serves 6

INGREDIENTS:

6 pork loin chops, about 6 ounces each

4 tsp. powdered cumin

2 tsp powdered cayenne pepper (to taste)

4 tsp. dried marjoram

6 cloves garlic, grated

2 tbsp. olive oil

Salt and pepper to season

Sliced lemons or oranges to garnish

DIRECTIONS:

1. Mix together all of the ingredients except the pork chops and garnish in a small bowl.

2. Rub the chops with this mixture and leave covered in the fridge for a few hours for the flavors to develop.

3. Heat a griddle to medium high and griddle the pork chops for 7 – 8 minutes on each side until cooked right through but still juicy.

4. Serve garnished with lemon or orange slices and seasonal vegetables of your choice.

STUFFED ACORN SQUASH

Serve on its own or with burger patties for an extra filling meal.

Serves 4

INGREDIENTS:

1 acorn squash

3 cups chopped celery

1 cup chopped onion

½ chopped red bell pepper

1½ cups apple sauce

Teaspoon mild curry powder

1 teaspoon cinnamon

1 tablespoon vegetable seasoning

14 ounces baby spinach

Salt and pepper to taste

DIRECTIONS:

1. Pre-heat the oven to 350°F. Place ¼ inch of water in the bottom of a baking tray.

2. Halve the squash and place cut side down on the baking sheet. Bake for 45 minutes until tender.

3. Stir together the apple sauce, curry, cinnamon and vegetable seasoning.

4. Turn the squash over when cooked and fill with the apple mixture. Bake for a further 10 minutes.

5. Steam the spinach until wilted. Serve the squash on a bed of spinach. Check the seasoning.

TINGLING TURKEY BURGERS

Make a comeback with these tasty, zingy turkey burgers! Make up an extra batch and freeze for an instant dinner!

Serves 6

INGREDIENTS:

2 pounds ground turkey meat

½ cup red onion, finely chopped

6 cloves garlic, finely chopped

½ tsp. chilli powder

½ tsp. ground black pepper

1 tsp. salt

2 tbsp. French mustard

½ cup almond flour

1 large fresh egg

DIRECTIONS:

1. Mix together all of the ingredients.

2. Shape into 12 patties with damp hands.

3. Heat a little olive oil in a frying pan over a medium heat.

4. Fry the burgers for 4 minutes on each side until cooked through.

5. Enjoy on wheat free buns or with a crisp green salad.

WALNUT AND GARLIC CHICKEN

Delicious and rich garlic sauce mixed with walnuts and chicken.

Serves 8

INGREDIENTS:

8 large chicken breasts, the meat taken off the bone

12 tbsp. olive oil

6 tbsp. walnuts, chopped

6 tbsp. parsley, chopped

6 cloves garlic, peeled and chopped

Salt and freshly ground black pepper

DIRECTIONS:

1. Preheat the oven at 400°F.

2. Place the chicken in an oven-proof serving dish.

3. Place all the remaining ingredients into a blender and Pulse into a sauce.

4. Spread the sauce on top of the chicken and bake in the oven for about 40 minutes, until the chicken becomes crispy and turns a fine golden color.

5. Serve the chicken with a fresh salad.

ZUCCHINI NOODLE SALAD

Here's an amazing and different way to serve zucchini – simple too! Use different herbs if you wish.

Serves 4

INGREDIENTS:

4 large zucchini

1 cup sundried tomatoes

2 cloves garlic

1 cup chopped fresh tomatoes

1 cup water

¼ cucumber, grated

3 tablespoons olive oil

1 tablespoon balsamic vinegar

¾ teaspoon each oregano, thyme and rosemary (fresh)

Sea salt to taste

DIRECTIONS:

1. Soak the sundried tomatoes in water for 20 minutes.

2. Meanwhile, shave the zucchini with a vegetable peeler to make thin, strip noodles.

3. Place the sundried tomatoes, when soaked, in a food processor, together with all of the other ingredients except the 'pasta'.

4. Process until smooth.

5. Mix into the zucchini and serve.

DESSERTS

ALMOND AND COCONUT COOKIES

These cookies have a lovely nutty flavor with delicious vanilla overtones.

Makes 24

INGREDIENTS:

1 cup butter, softened

1 cup erythritol

1½ cups coconut flour

4 medium fresh eggs

½ tsp. salt

¼ cup chopped almonds

1 tsp. vanilla extract

DIRECTIONS:

1. Pre-heat the oven to 375°F.

2. Line two cookie sheets with parchment paper.

3. In a medium sized bowl combine the sugar substitute, vanilla extract, salt and butter and beat well together.

4. Add the eggs one at a time, beating well after each addition.

5. Stir in the coconut flour.

6. Drop spoonfuls of the biscuit mix onto the prepared sheets, flatten with a fork.

7. Top with a sprinkle of chopped almonds and bake for 12 – 15 minutes in the hot oven.

8. Turn the cookies after 8 minutes to brown evenly.

9. Remove from the oven and cool on a wire rack.

BERRY SMOOTHIE

A refreshing mix of fruits, yogurt and ice to give your body a healthy boost!

Serves 2

INGREDIENTS:

1 cup coconut milk

1 cup full fat Greek yogurt

½ cup blueberries, blackberries, strawberries or other berries

1 cup gluten-free vanilla whey protein powder (gluten free)

2 tbsp. flaxseed, ground

1 tsp. coco extract

8 ice cubes

DIRECTIONS:

1. Combine all the ingredients then blend it until the texture is smooth.

2. Serve immediately.

BLUEBERRY AND VANILLA SMOOTHIE

This one could not be easier! Make sure you have plenty of blueberries in the freezer or switch it up with raspberries if you would prefer.

Serves 2

INGREDIENTS:

4 ounces vanilla low carb protein powder (gluten free)

4 cups frozen blueberries

1 pint of chilled water

DIRECTIONS:

1. Place all of the ingredients into a blender or smoothie maker.

2. Whizz up for about 30 seconds until nice a smooth.

3. Serve in a tall glass.

CHOCO-COCO CANDY BARS

You know you want to try this tummy tempter!

Makes about 8

INGREDIENTS:

6 tablespoons coconut oil

½ cup cocoa powder

1 cup ground hazelnuts

1½ cups unsweetened shredded coconut

2 tablespoons erythritol

DIRECTIONS:

1. Place the erythritol and the oil in a pan over a low heat until just warm and the coconut oil has melted.

2. Remove from the heat and stir in the cocoa, hazelnuts and coconut.

3. Mix well together.

4. Spoon onto a baking sheet lined with parchment paper and press down to form an even layer.

5. Mark with the back of a knife into 8 portions before placing in a fridge to harden once cool.

6. When the mixture has hardened cut through into 8 bars.

7. Place in a covered container in the fridge until ready to eat.

So easy and sure to leave you craving more – enjoy!

CHOCOLATE CUPCAKES

Top these with fresh strawberries or raspberries for a festive occasion!

Makes 12

INGREDIENTS:

2½ cups almond flour

2 tablespoons unsweetened cocoa

4 teaspoons baking soda

½ cups 80% dark chocolate chips

2 fresh farm eggs

4 tablespoons melted coconut oil

½ cup coconut milk – generous measure

2 tablespoons erythritol

1 cups 80% dark chocolate chips for the icing

12 tablespoons coconut milk

DIRECTIONS:

1. Pre-heat the oven to 350°F

2. Prepare 12 muffin cups with paper cases.

3. Mix together the flour, cocoa powder and the baking soda in a large bowl.

4. Melt the chocolate chips in a pan over a low heat and allow to cool for a few minutes.

5. Whisk the coconut oil, eggs, coconut milk and erythritol into the cooled chocolate.

6. Add the flour mixture to the chocolate and eggs and gently fold them together.

7. Spoon the mixture evenly between the muffin cases, filling each one to the top.

8. Bake for about 20 minutes until a tooth pick inserted into the middle comes out clean.

9. Remove from the oven and cool slightly before moving to a wire rack to cool completely.

10. While the cakes are cooling: melt the rest of the chocolate chips as before and mix in the coconut milk. Cool.

11. Ice the cup cakes.

Eat just as they are or decorate as desired. Sprinkle toasted nuts too – brilliant!

CHOCOLATE PEPPERMINT MOUSSE

Make this choc-minty pudding in small individual glass serve bowls – it looks amazing and just invites you to dig in! This is as close as it gets to an instant dessert.

Serves 4

INGREDIENTS:

1⅓ cups heavy cream, cold

¾ tsp. liquid stevia extract (adjust to taste)

½ tsp. peppermint extract

2 tbsp. unsweetened cocoa

2 ounces 80% dark chocolate, grated

Extra heavy cream, whipped for topping

DIRECTIONS:

1. Have ready the glass serve bowls by chilling in the fridge.

2. Place all of the ingredients in a large bowl and beat very well for a couple of minutes until fluffy.

3. Spoon into the cold dishes.

4. Top with a dollop of whipped cream and serve.

CHOCOLATE MERINGUES

Here's a chocolate variation on a meringue treat that you'll be able to enjoy with the entire family.

Makes 48

INGREDIENTS:

8 large fresh eggs, whites only

1 cup powdered erythritol

½ tsp. cream of tartar

4 tbsp. unsweetened cocoa powder

1 tsp. vanilla extract

3½ ounces 80% dark chocolate

1½ ounces butter

DIRECTIONS:

1. Pre-heat the oven to 200°F.

2. Line 2 cookie sheets with parchment paper.

3. Beat the egg whites with the cream of tartar until soft peaks form.

4. Mix the sugar substitute with the cocoa powder.

5. Slowly add the sugar substitute and cocoa mixture, beating well after each addition.

6. Continue beating until stiff peaks form.

7. Fold in the vanilla.

8. Spoon onto the prepared baking sheets.

9. Bake in the slow oven for 1 hour and 40 minutes.

10. Turn off the heat and leave the meringues to dry out for a further 3 hours or overnight.

11. When the meringues are crisp make the chocolate topping.

12. Melt the chocolate over low heat with the butter. Mix well.

13. Drizzle over the meringues. Leave to set.

CHOCOLATE SPRINKLED PUFFS

Puffed rice balls with chocolate and maple flavors!

Serves 8

INGREDIENTS:

2 ounces 80% dark chocolate chips

2 ounces butter

2 ounces puffed rice cereal

3 tbsp. unsweetened gluten-free cocoa powder

3 tbsp. sugar free maple syrup

DIRECTIONS:

1. Place 8 muffin cases in a baking tray

2. In a large sauce pan out the butter, cocoa powder, and syrup and melt over a low heat.

3. Remove the pan from the heat and stir in the chocolate chips. Stir and melt the majority of them

4. Add the puffed rice and stir until nicely coated.

5. Spoon equally into the muffin cases. Spoon any extra chocolate that might be left in the pan over the puffs.

6. Cool and serve.

CHOCOLATE TRUFFLES

Melt in your mouth chocolate morsels!

Makes 36

INGREDIENTS:

10 ounces 85% dark chocolate

3 tablespoons coconut oil

1 cup full fat coconut cream

1 teaspoon vanilla extract

Unsweetened toasted shredded coconut for finishing

DIRECTIONS:

1. Break up the chocolate and place in a heatproof bowl.

2. Add the coconut oil.

3. Place the bowl over a pan of simmering water and melt both gently together. Stir only gently with the tip of a knife.

4. When melted gently stir in the vanilla.

5. Warm the coconut cream gently over a low heat and add to the chocolate mixture. Fold carefully together.

6. Pour the truffle mixture into a sealed container and when cool refrigerate until solid – about 5 hours.

7. Spoon out the chocolate truffle mixture into your hands in walnut sized pieces. Form into balls and roll in the toasted coconut.

8. Serve on a glass plate or a special bonbon dish if you have one.

Keep these for a special occasion – they are worth it!

CHURRO WAFFLES

You will need a waffle iron to make these Spanish flavored treats.

Makes 6 small waffles

INGREDIENTS:

1½ cups ground almonds

½ teaspoon baking powder

Pinch of salt

1 teaspoon powdered cinnamon

Scant ½ cup unsweetened coconut milk

2 fresh farm eggs

1 tablespoon sugar free maple syrup

½ teaspoon vanilla extract

3 tablespoons butter - melted

Powdered erythritol to cover

DIRECTIONS:

1. Place all of the dry ingredients into a bowl and mix very well together.

2. In a separate bowl beat together the coconut milk, eggs, syrup and vanilla.

3. Add the egg mixture to the flour and mix well.

4. Heat a waffle iron.

5. Spoon the mixture in and cook through. If your waffle iron is not non-stick you may want to butter it first!

6. When all of the waffles are cooked, brush them with melted butter, dust them with powdered erythritol, and serve!

COCONUT APPLE BITES

Eat straight from the fridge for a summery fresh mouthful!

Makes 9

INGREDIENTS:

1 Granny Smith apple

½ cup creamed coconut

3 tablespoons coconut oil

3 teaspoons cinnamon powder

Pinch sea salt

Extra coconut oil for cooking

DIRECTIONS:

1. Place a silicon sheet on a baking sheet.

2. Soften the coconut oil and creamed coconut in a small pan over a low heat.

3. Core and dice the apple.

4. Place a small skillet on the stove and add 2 tablespoons coconut oil. Heat the pan to a medium temperature.

5. Toss in the chopped apple and cook down, caramelizing slightly. Do not burn it!

6. Once the apple is soft add the cinnamon and a pinch of salt.

7. Mix together the apple and the softened creamed coconut mixture.

8. Place spoonfuls of apple onto the silicon sheet.

9. Pop into the fridge for about half an hour to harden.

Keep these in the fridge or freezer, as they will melt quickly.

COCONUT CHEWS

Guess you are going to be caught dipping into these treats. Enjoy!

Makes 45

INGREDIENTS:

1½ ounces almond flour

¼ tsp. baking powder

Pinch salt

2 large eggs

1 tsp. vanilla extract

¼ tsp. almond extract

¾ cup erythritol

1 tbsp. butter, melted

8 ounces unsweetened coconut

DIRECTIONS:

1. Pre-heat the oven into 325°F.
2. Using baking parchment paper, line 2 cookie trays.
3. Mix together the flour, baking powder and salt in a bowl.
4. In a separate bowl mix together the eggs and extracts and beat well.
5. Beat the sugar substitute into the eggs. Blend in the melted butter.
6. Add the dry ingredients and then the coconut. Mix well.
7. Drop tablespoonfuls onto the parchment paper lined trays.
8. Put them close together as they do not spread.
9. Bake in the oven for 12 – 15 minutes until brown around the edges.

10. Be careful the chews do not burn.
11. Cool on a wire rack and serve.

COCONUT COOKIES WITH CHOCOLATE CHIPS

Awesome crunchy cookies – just irresistible!

Makes about 30 cookies

INGREDIENTS:

4 large fresh eggs

1 cup erythritol

¼ cup coconut butter

¼ cup coconut oil

1 tsp. vanilla essence

½ cup shredded unsweetened coconut

½ cup coconut flour

1 cup ground almonds

¼ tsp. baking soda

¼ tsp. salt

1 cup 80% dark chocolate chips

DIRECTIONS:

1. Preheat oven to 375°F.

2. Line a cookie sheet or two with parchment.

3. In a bowl whisk together the eggs, erythritol, coconut butter, oil and vanilla essence. Whisk until thoroughly combined.

4. Add shredded coconut, coconut flour, ground almonds, baking soda and salt.

5. Mix together until everything is completely combined.

6. Stir in chocolate chips.

7. Drop small spoonfuls of the cookie dough onto the prepared sheets.

8. Bake for about 18 minutes until brown and smelling delicious.

9. Leave to rest and form a little before removing the cookies to a cooling rack.

I'm imagining everyone turning into quite the little cookie monster after this batch is ready.

COCONUT CREAM POPSICLE

This is not just for the children – make enough for the whole family! Use an ice-lolly mold if you have or otherwise freeze in small narrow mugs and insert an ice-cream stick into each.

Makes 6

INGREDIENTS:

1 cup coconut cream

1 cup unsweetened macadamia milk

3 tbsp. unsweetened cocoa powder

1 tsp. vanilla extract

¼ tsp. liquid stevia extract (adjust to taste)

DIRECTIONS:

1. Place all of the ingredients except the sweetener in jug and blend until smooth.

2. Pour into 4 molds and place in the freezer. (Remember to put the sticks in!)

3. Freeze for several hours.

4. Enjoy!

COCONUT KEFIR

An amazing and unique drink which can be drunk on its own or blended with some fresh fruit into a smoothie!

Makes enough for 2 glasses

INGREDIENTS:

2 cans full fat coconut milk - chilled

3 capsules kefir, probiotic starter

8 teaspoons erythritol

Fresh fruit to serve

DIRECTIONS:

1. Place the coconut milk, probiotic starter and the erythritol in a blender and whizz around until well mixed.

2. Pour into a clean, dry, large glass jar.

3. Cover the jar with plastic wrap with some small holes in it.

4. Leave the jar in a warm place for about 3 days. Be patient. (You could also use a thermos flask)

5. Taste the kafir and it should be pleasantly sour and thick. If not, leave it a little longer.

6. Once the kafir is ready, place in the refrigerator, to chill for a few hours!

7. It is now ready to drink!

You can feel this doing you the world of good as you drink it!

GINGER MUFFINS

Muffins are always a firm favorite and these have a really exotic ginger taste you'll relish.

Makes 12

INGREDIENTS:

6 large fresh eggs, beaten

1 cup almond flour

3 tbsp. coconut flour

5 tbsp. grape seed oil

2½ ounces butter

1 tbsp. powdered ginger

1 tsp. baking powder

1 cup erythritol

½ tsp. salt

DIRECTIONS:

1. Pre-heat the oven to 350°F.

2. Prepare 12 muffin cups with paper cases.

3. Combine all of the dry ingredients in a medium bowl – mix well.

4. Add the egg, oil and butter to the dry ingredients and mix until smooth.

5. Divide among the prepared muffin cups and bake in the hot oven for 20 – 23 minutes.

6. When cooked remove from the oven and cool a little on a wire rack.

7. Serve warm.

LEMON CAKE

Enjoy this tangy cake that is firm but has a wonderful cake-like texture ideal for lemon lovers!

Serves 8- 10

INGREDIENTS:

8 ounces powdered erythritol

8 ounces butter

3 medium eggs, beaten

8 ounces ricotta cheese

5 ounces ground almonds

3½ ounces fine polenta

1 tsp. baking soda

4 ounces erythritol

3 lemons, juiced

⅓ cup water

3 ounces blueberries to decorate

DIRECTIONS:

1. Pre-heat the oven into 325°F.

2. Using a non-stick baking paper, line a 9 inch circular spring form cake tin.

3. Beat the butter and powdered erythritol in a large bowl until the texture becomes soft and creamy.

4. Beat in the eggs, ricotta cheese, ground almonds, polenta grains and baking soda thoroughly until it becomes smooth.

5. Spoon the mixture in the tin.

6. Place in the oven and bake for 60 to 90 minutes.

7. When the top is brown and the center firm remove from the oven.

8. While the cake is in the oven, create the lemon syrup.

9. Combine the remaining erythritol, water and juice from 3 freshly squeezed lemon in a small saucepan.

10. Boil the mixture and let it simmer for approximately 5 minutes until the texture becomes syrup like.

11. Place the ¾ of the lemon syrup onto the cake when it comes out of the oven and while it is still in the tin.

12. Cool the cake.

13. Once the cake is cooled completely, remove it from the tin and decorate it with the blueberries.

14. Spoon the remaining syrup on top of the cake and fruit.

LEMON FAT BOMBS

These use lemon juice and zest, for a blast of brain friendly coconut fats.

Makes 10

INGREDIENTS:

1 cup coconut oil

¼ cup butter

1 lemon, juiced plus the zest

½ tsp. liquid stevia extract (adjust to taste)

DIRECTIONS:

1. Prepare 10 small molds and place them on a baking sheet – heat resistant mini silicone muffin cases will do.

2. Combine the coconut oil and butter in a small saucepan and heat over a gentle heat until they become liquid.

3. Remove from heat, add the zest and lemon, and blend for a few minutes until smooth. The aim is for the lemon to start to set into the cooling mixture otherwise it will separate in the freezer.

4. Carefully pour into the prepared molds.

5. Freeze until required.

6. Store in the freezer!

MACADAMIA CHOCOLATE BARK WITH SEA SALT

Dark chocolate chunks with a nutty twist!

Make 20 small pieces

INGREDIENTS:

12 ounces of 80% dark chocolate

½ cup lightly toasted macadamia nuts

½ teaspoon sea salt flakes

DIRECTIONS:

1. Place the macadamia nuts into a processor and pulse a couple of times to chop them roughly.

2. Line a 4 pint square dish with parchment paper making sure that it comes up the side of the dish.

3. Break the chocolate into the top of a double boiler or into a heat proof bowl over a pan of simmering water.

4. Slowly melt the chocolate.

5. When melted add the chopped nuts and carefully mix. The nuts do not all have to be coated.

6. Spread the chocolate into the prepared dish, making sure that some of it goes up the side.

7. Sprinkle with the sea salt flakes.

8. Leave to set. Place in the fridge if the room is warm for about 10 minutes.

9. Remove the chocolate from the dish and snap into irregular sized small pieces.

MACADAMIA COOKIES

Crunchy cookies with just the right amount of nuts in every bite!

Makes 24 Cookies

INGREDIENTS:

14 ounces ground almonds

4 tbsp. erythritol

1 large egg

2 tsp. butter

1 tsp. pure vanilla extract

½ tsp. baking soda

Pinch of salt

4 ounces toasted macadamia nuts

DIRECTIONS:

1. Using a non-stick baking paper, line the 2 baking sheets

2. Place all of the ingredients except the nuts into a food processor. Pulse to combine.

3. Slowly add the macadamia nuts and whizz again.

4. Remove the dough from the processor, wrap in plastic wrap and put in the fridge for about 30 minutes to chill.

5. Pre-heat the oven into 375°F.

6. When the dough is ready divide into 24 balls and place on the cookie sheets. Press down with the back of a fork.

7. Place in the oven and bake for 10 – 12 minutes.

8. Remove from the oven and cool on a wire rack.

NUTTY MACAROONS

A favorite dessert biscuit made with a choice of nuts.

Makes 24 biscuits

INGREDIENTS:

2½ cups almonds or hazelnuts

¼ teaspoon of ground cinnamon

2 tablespoons unsweetened desiccated coconut

2 teaspoons of vanilla essence

4 egg whites

1 cup powdered erythritol

DIRECTIONS:

1. Preheat oven to 250°F.

2. Grind or chop the almonds or hazelnuts in a food processor. Leave a little grainy.

3. Mix cinnamon and vanilla in a medium bowl.

4. Whisk the egg whites and add to the cinnamon and vanilla.

5. Add the powdered erythritol and coconut and stir vigorously to blend thoroughly.

6. Add almond mixture and mix thoroughly.

7. Line a baking sheet with parchment paper.

8. Place teaspoonfuls of mixture on 2 baking sheets lined with parchment paper.

9. Bake for 30 minutes. Turn the trays after 20 minutes.

10. The Macaroons are ready when they are slightly brown.

11. Remove from the paper with a spatula while still slightly warm and place on a rack to cool completely.

PEANUT BUTTER COOKIES

A nutty butter cookie!

Makes 24 Cookies

INGREDIENTS:

4 ounces butter

6 ounces erythritol

4 ounces peanut butter

1 large egg, beaten

1 tsp. baking soda

6 ounces white rice flour

DIRECTIONS:

1. Pre-heat the oven into 350°F.

2. Line 2 cookie sheets with parchment paper.

3. In a large mixing bowl, beat the butter and erythritol and mix well.

4. Beat in the peanut butter and egg thoroughly.

5. Add the baking soda and rice flour.

6. Place spoonfuls the mixture on the cookie sheets evenly spaced, these cookies will spread during baking.

7. Bake for 18 – 22 minutes.

8. Remove once they turn golden brown.

9. Cool for a few minutes then transfer to cooling rack.

RICH CHOCOLATE CAKE

Enjoy a flourless cake that is great for dessert!

Serves 8-10

INGREDIENTS:

5 ounces butter

6 ounces 80% dark chocolate, chopped

5 medium eggs, separated

5 ounces powdered erythritol

3 tbsp. dark brewed coffee

3½ ounces ground almonds

2 tbsp. unsweetened gluten-free cocoa powder

1 tsp. baking soda

Gluten-free cocoa powder to dust

DIRECTIONS:

1. Pre-heat the oven to 375°F.

2. Line a 9 inch round cake tin with parchment.

3. Melt the chocolate pieces and butter in a saucepan over a low heat until they are completely melted and well combined.

4. Beat the egg white until it stiffens then add half of the erythritol and beat together.

5. Add the remaining erythritol into the egg yolks. Beat the mixture until it turns into a thick cream.

6. Gently stir together the combined melted chocolate, egg yolk mix and the coffee.

7. Gently fold the beaten egg whites into the mixture.

8. Combine the cocoa powder, baking soda, ground almonds and add it into the chocolate mix.

9. Pour the mixture into the tin.

10. Place the cake in the oven and bake it for 45 - 50mins, until firm.

11. Cool the cake for 30mins on the baking tin, and then transfer it to the wire cooling rack.

12. Dust with a sieved cocoa powder before serving.

SPICED APPLE CRUNCHIES

If you hanker after apple pie these cookies should fill your craving!

Makes 24

INGREDIENTS:

3 large Granny Smith apples

3 cups lightly toasted slivered almonds

3 teaspoons coconut oil

2 teaspoon vanilla extract

5 medium eggs

1½ cups desiccated unsweetened coconut

3 teaspoons erythritol

1 tablespoon mixed spice

Pinch of salt

DIRECTIONS:

1. Pre-heat the oven to 350°F.

2. Prepare to cookie sheets by covering them with parchment paper.

3. Peel and core the apples and grate them into a bowl and set aside.

4. Chop the almonds in a food processor. Mix in the spice, coconut oil, vanilla, salt and the erythritol.

5. In a large bowl combine the apple, the nut mixture and desiccated coconut.

6. Beat the eggs in a separate bowl, Add then to the apple mixture and mix well together.

7. Place spoonfuls of the dough onto the prepared baking sheets. Flatten each with a fork.

8. Bake for about 25 minutes in the centre of the oven until brown around the edges.

9. Turn the trays halfway through the baking.

10. Take out of the oven and cool on the sheets for a few minutes before cooling completely on a rack.

These smell SO.... good as they are cooking. You will be transported back to Granny's kitchen!

STRAWBERRY AND BANANA ICE

A dairy-free ice cream made with coconut milk and fresh chopped strawberries. Soooo good...

Serves 6

INGREDIENTS:

1 can full fat coconut milk (chilled in the fridge)

1 cup finely chopped strawberries

1 mashed ripe banana (medium)

1 teaspoons vanilla essence

¼ cup erythritol or to taste

DIRECTIONS:

1. Put the strawberries and the banana in a bowl.

2. Mix well together.

3. Add the coconut milk and combine well

4. Taste the mixture and add enough erythritol to give the desired sweetness.

5. Pour ice cream mixture into ice cream maker*. Follow the instructions for freezing.

6. *If you do not have an ice-cream maker place the mixture in a tray in a freezer and leave until ice crystals begin to form around the edges.

7. Pour into a bowl and beat the crystals well into the mixture. Pour back into the tray and refreeze. Repeat this process several times to achieve a delicious crystal free result.

8. Remove the ice cream from the freezer a short while before serving to allow it to soften a little.

9. Serve as is for a delicious desert or add fresh strawberries for that extra special occasion.

TANGY POLENTA CAKE

An orange cake with a Madeira texture!

Serves 8

INGREDIENTS:

3½ ounces butter

8 ounces powdered erythritol

8 ounces ground almonds

1 tsp. pure vanilla extract

3 medium eggs, beaten

7 ounces fine polenta

2 medium oranges, zested and juiced

1 tsp. baking soda

A pinch of salt

DIRECTIONS:

1. Pre-heat the oven into 375°F.

2. Using baking parchment paper, line a 9 inch cake tin (use a spring form tin for best result)

3. Beat the butter and erythritol together until light and fluffy.

4. Mix the ground almonds and vanilla into the mixture, stir well.

5. Add the eggs gradually, while continuously beating.

6. Stir in the polenta, orange zest, orange juice, baking soda and salt.

7. Spoon the mixture into the prepared tin and bake for 30 to 35 minutes.

8. Remove from the oven, cool and serve.

VANILLA CHUNKY ICE

A delicious ice cream with plenty of option to tweak as the fancy takes you.

Makes about 4 cups

INGREDIENTS:

1 can full fat coconut milk

4 egg yolks

3 tablespoons vanilla extract

5 tablespoons of erythritol

½ cup pureed strawberries or raspberries

½ cup unsweetened coconut flakes

¼ cup chopped toasted pecans or almonds

½ cup 80% dark chocolate chips

DIRECTIONS:

1. Prepare a double boiler or a large heatproof glass bowl over a pan of simmering water.

2. Pour the coconut milk into the bowl together with the vanilla and heat through until hot but not boiling.

3. Beat the egg yolks in a separate bowl

4. Add a few spoonfuls of the hot coconut milk to the eggs whisking well to incorporate the milk into the eggs.

5. Slowly pour in the rest of the hot milk while continuing to whisk it into the egg mixture.

6. Return the beaten egg and milk mixture to the large bowl or the top of the double boiler.

7. Continue whisking for a few minutes over the hot water until a thick egg custard like consistency is reached. Do not let the mixture get too hot or you will end up with scrambled eggs!

8. When thick remove from the heat and leave to cool completely.

9. Add the erythritol, puree and crunchy bits as desired.

10. Freeze until firm in an ice cream machine or in a dish in the freezer (stir every half an hour to ensure an icicle free texture).

11. Remove from the freezer a short while before serving to allow the ice cream to soften a little.

If prefer, add the fruit and nuts etc. after freezing as a topping for the plain vanilla ice cream! Utterly delicious!

VERY CHOCOLATY BROWNIES

Calling all chocolate lovers!

Makes 16

INGREDIENTS:

1¾ cups ground almonds

½ cup unsweetened gluten-free cocoa powder

½ cup sliced almonds

2 ounces 80% dark chocolate chips

½ tsp. baking soda

Pinch of salt

6 tbsp. boiling water

2 large eggs

1 cup coconut milk

2 tsp. pure vanilla extract

½ cup coconut oil

15 drops liquid stevia

DIRECTIONS:

1. Pre-heat the oven to 350°F.

2. Line a baking tin with parchment 11 inches x 7 inches.

3. In a large bowl combine the ground almonds, cocoa, chocolate chips, baking soda, sliced almonds and salt.

4. Stir well together.

5. In a separate bowl mix together the coconut milk, vanilla, melted coconut oil and stevia.

6. Add to the dry ingredients, stirring well to combine.

7. Pour the mixture into the prepared baking tray.

8. Place in the oven and bake for about 45 minutes.

9. Check that the brownies do not get too dry.

10. Remove the tray from the oven and leave to sool for about half an hour.

11. Slice into 16 pieces. Serve

YIN-YANG CHOC VANILLA DIP

Slather a strawberry with this fondue-esque dip.

Makes 2 Dips

INGREDIENTS:

1 cup coconut milk

2 bananas

1 teaspoon vanilla

2 teaspoons coconut flour

1½ teaspoons of non-sweet cocoa powder

DIRECTIONS:

1. Add everything except the cocoa to a processor, and blend until smooth and silky.

2. Pour half of the mixture into a serving bowl.

3. Add the cocoa powder to the remaining mixture and continue processing until the powder has mixed through.

4. Pour the chocolate mixture into a 2nd serving bowl.

5. Refrigerate the mixtures to thicken them up!

Where is that pancake recipe gone? I think it's time to introduce this liquid heaven and several strawberries to my stomach!

STRAWBERRY AND CHOCOLATE SMOOTHIE

A taste of summer all year round if you fancy it! The classic taste of chocolate and strawberries! What a pleasure!

Serves 2

INGREDIENTS:

4 ounces of chocolate low carb protein powder (gluten free)

4 cups frozen strawberries

2 tablespoons coconut oil

1 pint iced water

DIRECTIONS:

1. Place all of the ingredients into a blender or processor

2. Blend for 30 seconds or more so as to produce a smooth mixture.

3. Serve.

THANK YOU

If you enjoyed this, and I'm guessing your taste buds did, please keep an out for some of the other recipe books I've created!

Thanks so much to my family, and friends, and to all those pursuing healthy living within the gluten-free, low carb community.

Be good to each other!

Piper Reynolds

Made in the USA
Middletown, DE
10 December 2014